Planet Earth
GEMSTONES

TIME LIFE BOOKS

Other Publications:

THE ENCHANTED WORLD
THE KODAK LIBRARY OF CREATIVE PHOTOGRAPHY
GREAT MEALS IN MINUTES
THE CIVIL WAR
COLLECTOR'S LIBRARY OF THE CIVIL WAR
LIBRARY OF HEALTH
CLASSICS OF THE OLD WEST
THE EPIC OF FLIGHT
THE GOOD COOK
THE SEAFARERS
WORLD WAR II
HOME REPAIR AND IMPROVEMENT
THE OLD WEST
LIFE LIBRARY OF PHOTOGRAPHY (revised)
LIFE SCIENCE LIBRARY (revised)

For information on and a full description of any of
the Time-Life Books series listed above, please write:
   Reader Information
   Time-Life Books
   541 North Fairbanks Court
   Chicago, Illinois 60611

This volume is one of a series that examines the
workings of the planet earth, from the geological
wonders of its continents to the marvels of its
atmosphere and its ocean depths.

Cover
A red tourmaline from Brazil is framed by a
white ruff of the mineral albite in which
the gemstone formed. The vertical striations are
typical of natural tourmaline crystals, which
surpass all other gems in their range of colors.

Planet Earth

GEMSTONES

By Paul O'Neil
and The Editors of Time-Life Books

Time-Life Books, Alexandria, Virginia

PLANET EARTH

EDITOR: Thomas A. Lewis
Deputy Editor: Russell B. Adams Jr.
Designer: Albert Sherman
Chief Researcher: Patti H. Cass

Editorial Staff for *Gemstones*
Associate Editor: Neil Kagan (pictures)
Text Editors: Tim Appenzeller, Paul N. Mathless
Staff Writers: William C. Banks, Jan Leslie Cook,
Thomas H. Flaherty Jr.
Researchers: Jean Crawford, Blaine Marshall
(principals), Susan S. Blair, John S. Marshall,
Barbara Moir
Assistant Designer: Susan K. White
Copy Coordinators: Elizabeth Graham,
Anthony K. Pordes
Picture Coordinator: Renée DeSandies
Editorial Assistant: Caroline A. Boubin

Special Contributor: Champ Clark (text)

Editorial Operations
Design: Ellen Robling (assistant director)
Copy Room: Diane Ullius
Production: Anne B. Landry (director), Celia Beattie
Quality Control: James J. Cox (director), Sally Collins
Library: Louise D. Forstall

Correspondents: Elisabeth Kraemer-Singh (Bonn);
Margot Hapgood, Dorothy Bacon (London); Miriam
Hsia, Lucy T. Voulgaris (New York); Maria Vincenza
Aloisi, Josephine du Brusle (Paris); Ann Natanson
(Rome). Valuable assistance was also provided by:
Lesley Coleman, Millicent Trowbridge (London);
John Dunn (Melbourne); Felix Rosenthal (Moscow);
Christina Lieberman (New York); Patricia Robb (Rio
de Janeiro); Ann Wise (Rome).

Library of Congress Cataloguing in Publication Data
O'Neil, Paul, 1909-
　Gemstones.
　(Planet earth)
　Bibliography: p.
　Includes index.
　1. Precious stones. I. Time-Life Books. II. Title.
III. Series.
QE392.O53 1983　　553.8　　83-602
ISBN 0-8094-4500-X
ISBN 0-8094-4501-8 (lib. bdg.)

THE AUTHOR

Paul O'Neil became a freelance writer in 1973
after a 30-year career as a staff writer for *Time,
Sports Illustrated* and *Life.* He is the author of
three volumes in the Time-Life series The Old
West and more recently wrote *Barnstormers and
Speed Kings* in the Epic of Flight series.

THE CONSULTANTS

Paul E. Desautels is an internationally known
gemologist and a former curator of the Department of Mineral Sciences at the Smithsonian Institution's National Museum of Natural History. He is also a popular lecturer and the author of
several publications including *The Gem Kingdom*
and *The Mineral Kingdom.*

Dr. Peter C. Keller is Director of Education at
the Gemological Institute of America in Santa
Monica, California, and associate editor of its
journal, *Gems & Gemology.* A recognized authority on gem deposits, he has published numerous
articles on gemstone mining around the world.

CONTENTS

RICHES IN THE ROCKS

Gemstones, prodigally gifted with radiance and color, seem to stand apart from the common workings of nature. The ancients thought gems were of supernatural origin and ascribed to them all manner of powers. According to the Greeks, a goblet made of amethyst could ward off drunkenness; the Burmese believed that a ruby sewed into the flesh would make a warrior invulnerable.

By the 17th Century, scientists had come to understand gems as "rare and noble productions of nature," in the words of the English physicist Robert Boyle. They are distilled from duller rock by processes that often involve the play of fierce heat and pressure deep within the earth's crust. And they derive their loveliness from a variety of prosaic sources. For example, precious ruby and the common abrasive emery consist of the same basic mineral, corundum; the difference between them is accounted for by the presence of minute traces of other substances. Diamond is chemically identical to graphite; only a different crystalline structure gives diamond the hardness, clarity and flash for which it is so highly esteemed.

Beauty, durability and rarity are the distinguishing traits of gemstones. The number of minerals accorded that status varies with circumstances of fashion and availability, but the 15 shown here and on the following pages are the most universally valued.

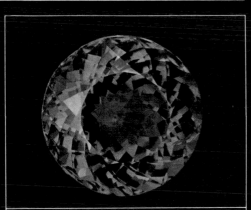

TOURMALINE
Six-inch rods of tourmaline rise from the matrix of other minerals with which they formed (*left*). The wide variety of rich hues that make tourmaline a spectacular cut gem (*above*) is due to minute differences in chemical composition.

AMETHYST

Intergrown crystals of amethyst *(below)*, the most valuable of the many forms of quartz, may derive their color from minute traces of iron. Quartz is abundant, but large, evenly colored amethysts of gem quality *(above)* are scarce.

TOPAZ.
An eight-inch crystal of topaz (*right*), encrusted with another mineral, lepidolite, shimmers pale blue; other topaz hues include pink, red, yellow and brown. Cut topaz (*above*) is prized for its brilliance as well as its color.

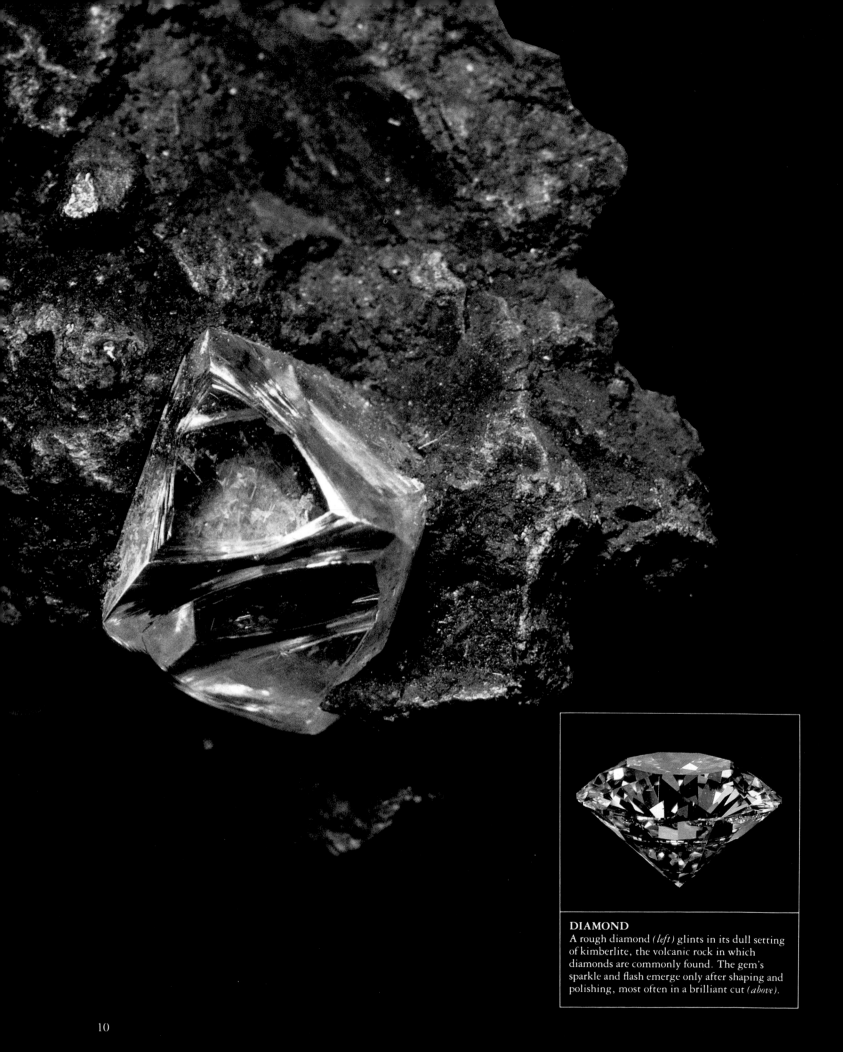

DIAMOND
A rough diamond (*left*) glints in its dull setting of kimberlite, the volcanic rock in which diamonds are commonly found. The gem's sparkle and flash emerge only after shaping and polishing, most often in a brilliant cut (*above*).

TANZANITE
Named for the country of Tanzania, where it is mined, tanzanite has been esteemed as a gem only since the 1960s. An uncut stone *(left)* displays regular crystalline faces that rival the facets of a cut tanzanite *(above)*.

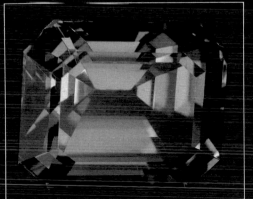

TSAVORITE
A form of the common mineral grossular garnet, tsavorite is more durable, a purer green and, in cut form *(above)*, more sparkly than emerald. It is also rarer and is found in rough chunks like the ones pictured at right.

11

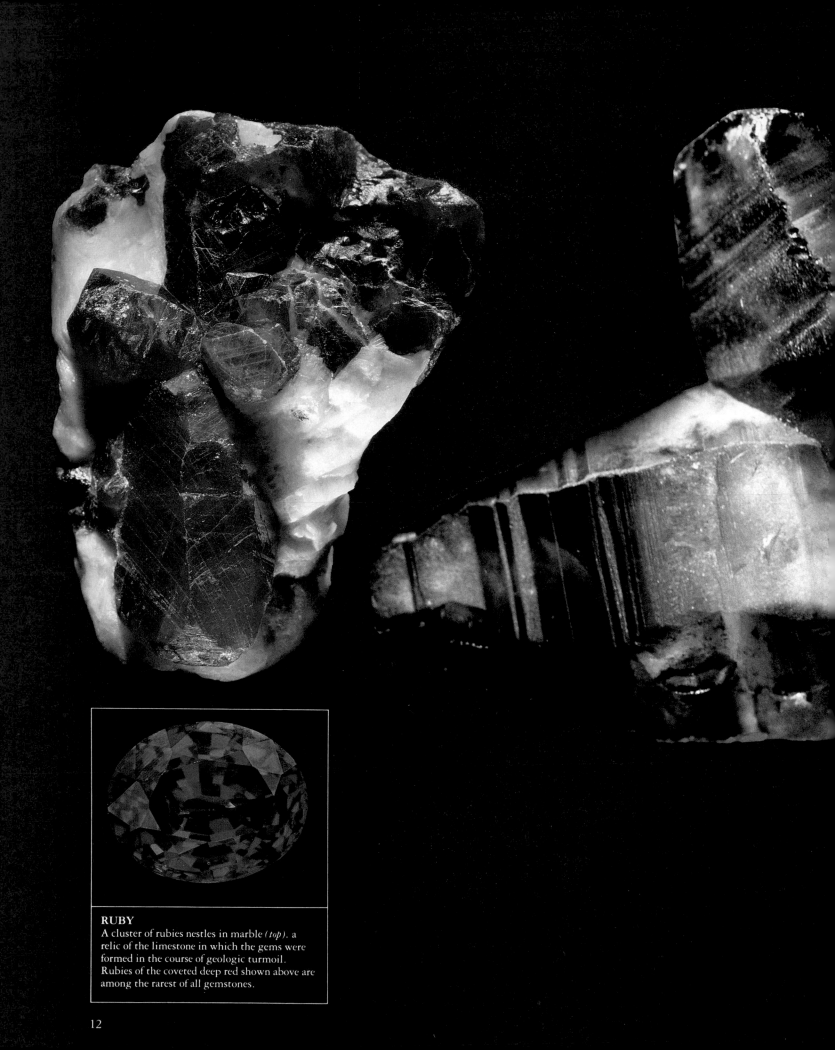

RUBY
A cluster of rubies nestles in marble (*top*), a
relic of the limestone in which the gems were
formed in the course of geologic turmoil.
Rubies of the coveted deep red shown above are
among the rarest of all gemstones.

SAPPHIRE
Sapphire occurs in various colors, including green, orange and yellow, but the most desirable shade is the blue of the one-and-a-half-inch crystal cluster below and the cut gem above. Like ruby, sapphire is a variety of corundum.

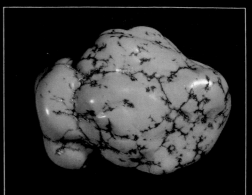

TURQUOISE
Veins of turquoise lace a pebble found in China
(*left*). Because turquoise is soft and opaque, it is
never faceted but is simply shaped and polished
(*above*) to display its waxy luster and fine blue
color, the result of its copper content.

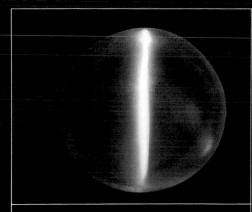

CHRYSOBERYL
Crystals of chrysoberyl form a six-rayed mineral snowflake about two inches across *(right)*. A type of chrysoberyl called a cat's-eye *(above)* reflects a glowing band of light from thousands of microscopic parallel threads of impurity.

LAPIS LAZULI
A four-inch chunk of lapis lazuli — the name means "blue stone" — is flecked with yellow pyrite *(left)*. An opaque mixture of minerals, lapis is prized for its color and is displayed without elaborate facets *(above)*.

EMERALD
An uncut emerald three and a half inches high glows a rich green (*left*), the result of traces of chromium in the mineral. The polished emerald above is cut in the style most often used for transparent colored gems.

AQUAMARINE

The shades of aquamarine — all caused by traces of iron — range from the blue-green of the two-and-three-quarter-inch uncut crystal below to the pale blue of the cut gem above. Like emerald, aquamarine is a variety of beryl.

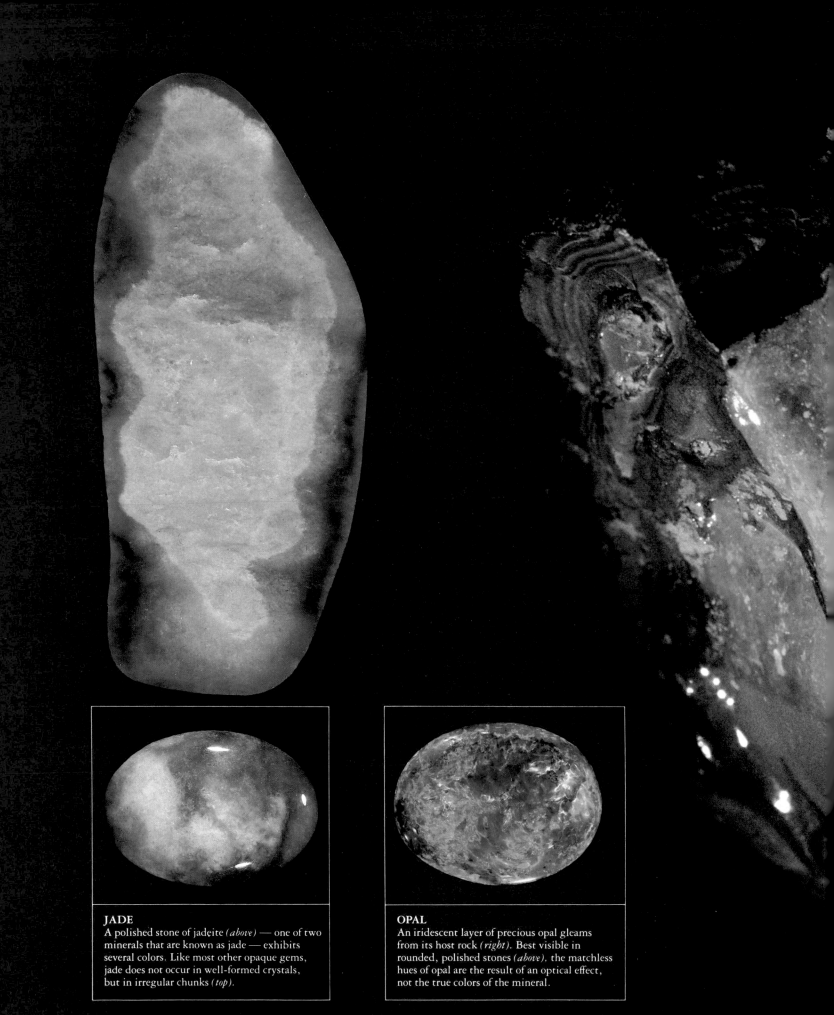

JADE
A polished stone of jadeite *(above)* — one of two minerals that are known as jade — exhibits several colors. Like most other opaque gems, jade does not occur in well-formed crystals, but in irregular chunks *(top)*.

OPAL
An iridescent layer of precious opal gleams from its host rock *(right)*. Best visible in rounded, polished stones *(above)*, the matchless hues of opal are the result of an optical effect, not the true colors of the mineral.

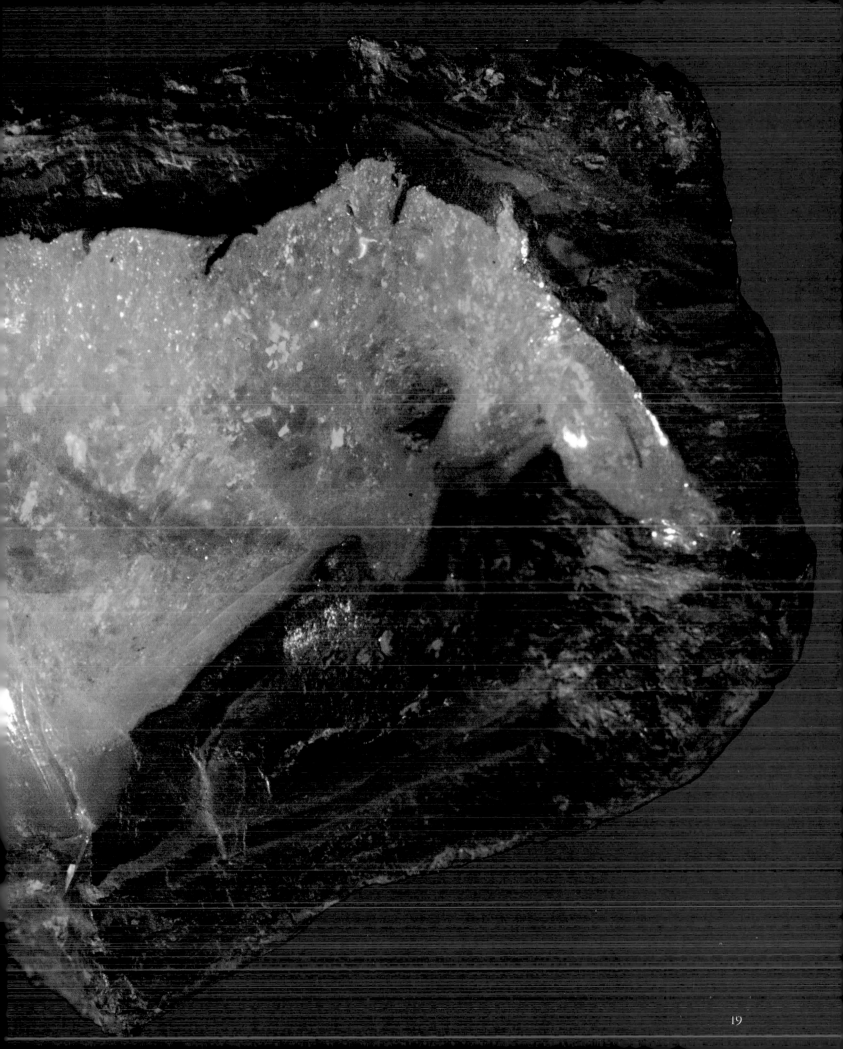

"THE FLOWERS OF THE KINGDOM"

The diamond is the most precious of all stones, and it is the article of trade to which I am most devoted. In order to acquire a thorough knowledge of it I resolved to visit all the mines, and one of the two rivers where it is found; and as the fear of dangers has never restrained me in any of my journeys, the terrible picture that was drawn of these mines, as being in barbarous countries to which one could not travel except by the most dangerous routes, served neither to terrify me nor to turn me from my intention."

In this fashion, Jean Baptiste Tavernier, a plump little Parisian of great courage and curiosity, described how one day in 1645 he came to be standing on a hill in India, then the world's principal diamond supplier. Tavernier was visiting the mines of Coulour, not far from the city of Golconda, a place so renowned for gems that its very name remains a synonym for enormous wealth. From his vantage point the Frenchman could see below him 60,000 laborers of all ages, lashed by their overseers' whips, scrabbling after diamonds under the scorching sun. "The men fall to digging," he reported, "and the women and children to carrying the earth to a place enclosed in a wall about two feet high with small holes to let in water they stop up afterwards. They let it soak for two or three days until it comes to be a kind of batter. Then they open up the holes till the mud is washed away and nothing left but sand. This they dry in the sun and winnow as we winnow our corn, and, spreading it with a rake, they look for the diamond."

Tavernier's tour of India's mines, the first by a European, was but one of many high points in the career of this remarkable gem connoisseur and merchant, who for 40 years, beginning in 1631, wandered the mysterious and often perilous Far East in search of jewels. "A man cannot travel in Asia as they do in Europe," he wrote. "There are no weekly coaches. There are no certain inns to entertain travelers. There are vast deserts to cross and very dangerous, both for want of water and the robberies that Arabs commit daily therein. As for Turkey, it is full of thieves that keep in troops together and waylay merchants upon the roads and will certainly rob them, nay many times murder them, if they are not guarded very well."

Yet Tavernier not only survived, he flourished mightily, and his memory remains bright after more than 300 years. He is remembered by history partly because his daring journeys opened European eyes to the exotic world of the Orient — and partly because his avid pursuit of gemstones celebrates one of the most powerful urges of mankind.

Driven by a compulsion to possess tiny bits of shiny stone that were (at least until the advent of modern technology) utterly useless in themselves,

In an 18th Century miniature, a Mogul Emperor sits upon the fabled Peacock Throne. Encrusted with diamonds, rubies, emeralds, sapphires and pearls — an accumulation of gems only dreamed of in the West — the throne came to symbolize the sumptuous wealth of the Orient.

men have crossed oceans and deserts, scaled mountains and dived beneath the surface of the sea; they have schemed and plotted, lied and stolen, fought wars and suffered agonies of torture; they have killed and they have been killed. Diamonds, rubies, emeralds and sapphires have throughout history been the most highly prized of the family of coveted gemstone species. But after them comes a gleaming procession of amethyst, alexandrite and aquamarine, garnet, jade, opal, tourmaline and turquoise and topaz, zircon and scores of others. Each has brought a special flash of beauty to the long and often dark course of human affairs.

Although the genesis of mankind's passion for gems has vanished in the mists of prehistory, the modern excavation of an ancient lake dweller's grave in Czechoslovakia uncovered several garnet pebbles in which small holes had been made, strongly suggesting that Bronze Age people were adorning themselves with gemstone beads 5,000 years ago. And by the time of the Old Testament prophet Ezekiel, in the Sixth Century B.C., gemstones were already so firmly fixed in legend that carnelian, topaz, jasper, chrysolite, beryl, onyx, garnet, sapphire and emerald were listed in the Bible as being among the natural blessings bestowed on the ill-fated couple in "Eden, the garden of God."

The cataclysmic forces that shape the earth have been generous in producing such basic sources of wealth as iron, granite, marble, copper, coal, petroleum, and the soils that nurture forests and crops. But they have been woefully stingy in the creation of gemstones. Only when certain constituent elements of the earth's molten inner magma have combined under enormous pressure in precise proportions, and then cooled and solidified at a certain rate, has the result included a comparative handful of crystals whose inner fire, or radiance, or rainbow hues make them desirable as articles of jewelry. Even then, with rare exceptions, these anomalous and negligible bits of matter have been enclosed, at least in the beginning, within countless tons of commoner stuff.

Only when their surrounding rock was thrust to the surface during the birth of mountain ranges, and then eroded away by rain, wind, frost and heat, were the gems free to begin their long waterborne journeys to the river-valley gravel beds where most of them were first discovered. Yet for all the obscurity of their origins and for all their rarity, these flashing pebbles have played a continuing and commanding role in human history, and there is no sign that they will soon relinquish their grip on the human spirit. Diamonds today provide the foundation for a global corporate empire that employs modern technology and marketing methods that the 17th Century merchant Tavernier could not have imagined. While in dramatic contrast, the finding and fashioning of such colored crystals as rubies, sapphires and emeralds, by men, women and children who labor in some of the world's most pestilential places, remains an enterprise with which Jean Baptiste Tavernier would have been instantly familiar.

A love of far places was instilled in the young Tavernier by the maps he studied as a boy in the printing establishment of his father, a wealthy geographer and engraver. The young man was determined to see these places for himself, and he prepared for a life of travel by becoming expert in geography and foreign languages. Although the family fortune was ample, he established himself as a merchant, the better to move easily from place to

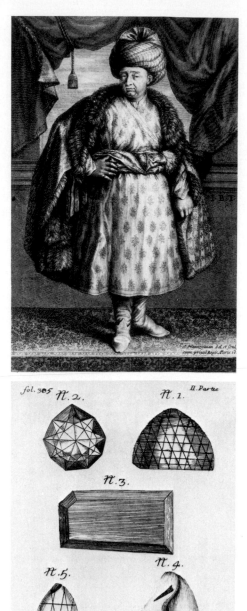

Jean Baptiste Tavernier (*top*), the pioneer French trader in fine gems, wears a robe of silk and fur presented to him by a 17th Century Indian ruler. At bottom, an engraving from Tavernier's account of his travels, *Six Voyages*, illustrates some of the great diamonds he saw while he was in the Orient.

place, and to gain the confidence of important personages. But he was never as interested in profit as he was in acquiring knowledge. By the time he was 22 he had toured most of Europe; then, irresistibly drawn, he set out on the first of his six voyages to India.

"Our noble Tavernier," wrote an English admirer in 1680, "had money in abundance and a prince's retinue, without which none are deemed fit for admittance into great and worthy companies in luxurious Asia." By the same account he was "an obliging traveler with a graceful countenance so that he got into the presence of emperors and of ministers of state." Tavernier traveled heavy-laden with a variety of enticing articles, such items as pocket watches from France and telescopes and decorative boxes from Italy, which he used to ingratiate himself with India's fiercely acquisitive nabobs. But such items could accomplish no more than gain him entry to the royal courts; after that, the hard trading began. "It is not enough," he wrote, "to carry such trifles to truck for diamonds; these people will not only have gold but gold of the best sort, too."

Carrying gold about the Indian countryside was of course a chancy undertaking, and Tavernier did his best to cut the risk by engaging a native bodyguard of "twenty or thirty outriders armed with bows and arrows and some with muskets." Thus escorted, he went about his business in style, riding in a coach drawn by oxen that had cost him "near six hundred rupees" and could "travel fifteen leagues a day upon the trot with a pace as easy as our hackneys if given two or three balls of wheat kneaded up with butter."

Even when circumstances demanded that he abandon his comfortable little coach, Tavernier tried to maintain certain amenities. On one occasion he accompanied a sultan's army into the parched Indian hinterlands. With his usual foresight, he provided himself with "two good Tartarian horses, a tent of the middle size, a little bed made up of light canes with a pillow for the head, two coverlets, napkins of dyed cloth, plates and a round table-cloth of leather to eat upon." Besides a groom and a cook, his retinue included a servant "to march before the horse with a flagon of water in his hand" so the animal would not suffer from thirst.

Despite such commendable care for Tavernier's own needs, the expedition was uncomfortable in the extreme. "My body has become a sieve, very dry," he wrote miserably in a letter. "I have no sooner taken into my stomach a pint of water (for less will not serve) than I see it issue out of my limbs like dew. The sun is intolerable. My face and hands are peeled off. All my hope is in a little dry curdled milk which I am going to dilute with water and lemons. I know not in the morning whether I should live until night. Farewell. The ink dries at the end of my pen and the pen falls out of my hand."

Tavernier was a bit of a dramatist. His discomfort did not prevent him from working his way into the good graces of the army's commander, India's Mogul of Moguls, the treacherous and deadly Aurangzeb. After seizing power by imprisoning his father and having his three brothers assassinated, the new monarch became the proud inventor of a hooked device that he could wear as a glove to disembowel those unfortunate subjects who displeased him. Yet so far as Tavernier was concerned, Aurangzeb had one greatly redeeming virtue: He owned the world's most fabulous collection of jewels. And in the autumn of 1665, Jean Baptiste Tavernier reached the esthetic apogee of his inquisitive career by becoming the first European to view the Mogul's treasure — or, at least, part of it.

It took some doing. Tavernier first had to earn an invitation to the five-day feast at which Aurangzeb, celebrating his birthday, annually received magnificent gifts from the nobles of the realm. Carpets, rare fabrics, camels, horses and elephants were deemed acceptable, but those who were truly intent on royal preference gave great gems. Tavernier resorted to broad-scale bribery, which he recounted in detail in his journal. He gave the Mogul's uncle a ruby ring and a Florentine cabinet worked with gemstones in designs representing birds and flowers. To the royal treasurer went "a gold watch set with emeralds, to the Eunuch of Aurangzeb's sister, a watch in a painted case, and to the Porter of the Treasury, two hundred rupees."

As for the Mogul himself, he got "a buckler of brass, richly gilt and wrought by the best workmen in France by order of Cardinal Richelieu, a battle ax of crystal set with rubies and emeralds and encased in gold; and a saddle and cloth embroidered in gold and silver."

The experience was worth the cost, and even the worldly Tavernier could only marvel at such wonders as the famed Peacock Throne, "formed like a field bed, six feet long and four broad," upon which the monarch reclined on ceremonial occasions. The gaudy seat of state took its name from a bejeweled peacock of beaten gold that roosted, tail spread, atop a canopy surmounting the throne's bolster and cushions. The canopy was embroidered with pearls and diamonds, the bird's tail was "all of sapphires" and its breast boasted a magnificent ruby. In the throne itself, Tavernier (who was always precise about such things) counted 108 rubies, the least of which weighed 100 carats — just under one ounce — and 116 big emeralds.

"When the king seats himself," Tavernier wrote, "there is a diamond of ninety carats encompassed with rubies and emeralds so hung that it is always in his eye. And behind this stately throne there is a lesser one in the form of a tub in which the king bathes himself. It is an oval, seven feet long and four broad. The outside shines all over with diamonds and pearls, but there is no canopy over it."

Before the birthday festivities were done, Tavernier was admitted to the sanctum where Aurangzeb's jewels were kept. There, Akil Khan, keeper of the gems, ordered four eunuchs to fetch two "large wooden trays lacquered with gold leaf, one covered with red velvet and the other with green brocade." A long precautionary ritual ensued. The contents of boxes on the trays were carefully counted and listed by one scribe, again by another scribe and once more by a third. Tavernier swallowed his impatience: "These Indians do everything with great circumspection and, if anyone becomes angry, smile as at a madman."

He was finally and fully rewarded by the awesome sight of thousands of jewels of all species, shapes and sizes, the least of them worth the ransom of a prince if not of a king. The visual feast included a topaz of 158 carats, a handful of spectacular diamonds, and chains of rubies and pearls. Then, recalled Tavernier, as the grand climax, "Akil Khan put into my hands a great diamond, round rose cut and very high on one side. Its water is beautiful and it weighs 280 of our carats." Surprisingly, Tavernier's enthusiasm for the enormous gem — known as the Great Mogul — was tempered. The artisan who had fashioned the diamond from a giant stone weighing no less than 787 carats had butchered the job. The final product resembled, in

A necklace of pre-19th Century Indian design features 24 polished but unfaceted emeralds and 47 smaller emerald beads on a chain covered with tiny diamonds. A hole has been drilled in each emerald and a wire passed through to attach the gem securely to the chain.

Tavernier's scornful words, "half of an egg, cut in the middle." In fact Aurangzeb had been so outraged at the result he had not only refused to pay the diamond cutter, but had imposed a stiff fine as a penalty.

Nevertheless, the Great Mogul was very probably the largest diamond in the world, and if Tavernier was less than enraptured by it he may have had in mind its distressingly brief and ordinary history: It had been found only a few years before in India's renowned Golconda diamond fields, and had been rather routinely presented to Aurangzeb's father during his abbreviated reign. To Jean Baptiste Tavernier, a gem without history was of little more than passing interest.

Tavernier was heir to centuries of gemstone lore, and he did well by his inheritance of knowledge, increasing it greatly in his travels and his trading. In his time the science of gemology was as yet unborn, and diamond colors were classified by comparison with clear stream water — the finest stones were colorless and known as gems of the first water. "Indians," he wrote, "judge the water of stones and the specks in them by holding them between their fingers at night before a lamp with a large wick they set in a hole about a foot square in the wall." As often happened, Tavernier devised a better method. "The most infallible way," he insisted, "is to carry a stone under a tree thick with boughs during the day, for in that shade you may easily discern whether the water be bluish or no."

By that technique of avoiding direct light and hence reducing the surface glitter of a diamond, Tavernier made unwitting application of the modern science of optics — the study of the phenomena involved in the interplay between light and material substances.

In 1668, three years after he had inspected Aurangzeb's treasures, Tavernier left India forever. Returning to Europe, he settled down to enjoy the wealth and the fame that had accrued to him. But two decades later, at the age of 83, he once more answered the call of the East and set out for Persia. This time he went overland, for some reason going by way of Moscow, where he died — according to at least one account — after being attacked by a pack of wolves.

Although he had found time to marry at the age of 56, Tavernier had no children, and in any case would have been able to bequeath to them very little; his nephew, who had been involved in Tavernier's business affairs in the East, had managed to squander the fortune that had been entrusted to him. But the far-ranging traveler's true legacy was the wealth of lore he passed on to succeeding generations, and he would have delighted in what the future held for some of the great gems he knew.

The marvelous Peacock Throne, for example, fell into the hands of Nadir Shah, a soldier of fortune who made himself the ruler of Persia, invaded India and, after brushing aside two armies that had been sent to contest his passage, entered Delhi in March of 1739, at the head of his victorious troops. After some resentful Indians killed one of his aides and threw some stones in his direction, Nadir Shah ordered a day-long massacre in which his soldiers slaughtered 30,000 men, women and children. Then he settled down to the pleasures of looting, and carried off a treasure in gold, silver, plate and other valuables beyond computation.

Thus the Peacock Throne came to Persia, where it became the predominant symbol of royal authority and wealth. The fate of the throne is clouded

The magnificently plumed Pahlavi crown, made for the 1926 coronation of Riza Shah the Great, is mounted with a profusion of diamonds, pearls, sapphires and emeralds — thousands in all. The eight-inch-high crown survives as part of the national treasure of Iran.

by contradictory accounts of a number of reconstructions and duplications of the original, but the reproduction used most recently by the late Shah Muhammed Riza Pahlavi was studded with 26,733 gems and, along with innumerable crowns, scepters, tiaras, necklaces and heaps of loose gems, was stored at the Central Bank of Iran as the basis of the national currency. Much to their resentment, members of the Royal Family, including Empress Soraya, were required to sign chits to use the crown jewels and to return them promptly after they had been worn. When the Ayatollah Khomeini ended the Pahlavi regime, there was no further demand for ceremonial use of the jewels, but their role as support for the currency continued.

In addition to the Peacock Throne, Nadir Shah also pilfered a huge diamond that, although it had undoubtedly belonged to Aurangzeb, seems to have escaped Tavernier's avid gaze. Had he seen it, he would certainly have gone into ecstasies, not so much over its beauty, for it lacks the fire of a truly great diamond, as over its long and bloodstained history.

Although many of the details are lost, the gem may be the oldest of all known diamonds. It was found more than 5,000 years ago, celebrated in an ancient Sanskrit epic, the *Mahabharata,* and seized from the Rajah of Malwa by Sultan Ala-ad-Din in 1304. It fell into the hands of Baber, first of the Great Moguls, when he invaded northern India from Afghanistan in 1526. "It is so valuable," Baber recorded in his diary, "that it would pay half the daily expenses of the whole world."

Baber's descendant, the ferocious Aurangzeb, was more than capable of protecting the diamond and passing it on to his own heirs. But Aurangzeb's great-grandson, Muhammad Shah, was a far less formidable man.

When the Persian invader Nadir Shah heard of the stone, he was, of course, determined to have it. Yet though he set his minions to searching

A map of the world's major deposits of gemstones shows them dispersed unevenly across six continents. Whether there are substantial finds to be made in Antarctica is still unknown.

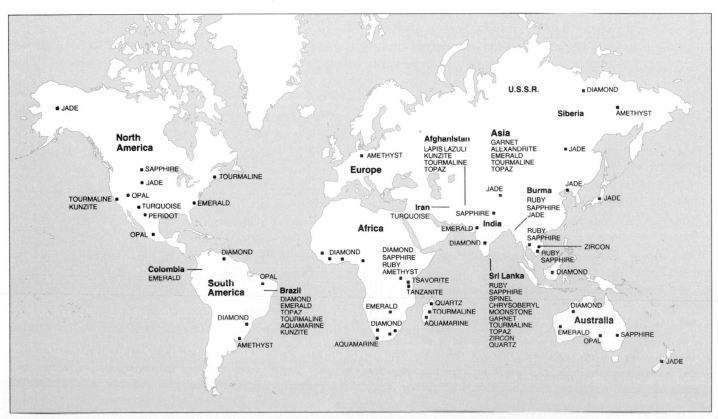

high and low, it was nowhere to be found, until a treacherous woman of the Indian mogul's harem revealed that Muhammad Shah was keeping the gem concealed in his turban.

That posed a problem. Although Nadir Shah could easily have taken the turban, and for that matter Muhammad Shah's head as well, he was a social climber of sorts. Of lowly birth, he had decided to improve his family's status by marrying one of his sons to a daughter of Muhammad Shah. To murder the boy's future father-in-law would have been a definite breach of etiquette, even given the violence common to the time and place. Clearly, then, Nadir Shah would have to resort to trickery.

He rose to the occasion at a grand state banquet by praising Muhammad Shah to the heavens and then suggesting that, as a gesture of good will and mutual respect, they trade turbans. By prevailing custom, refusal was unthinkable, and the transaction took place. Returning to his private quarters, Nadir Shah unwound the yards of cloth that formed Muhammad's turban, and out tumbled the diamond. *"Koh-i-noor!"* cried Nadir Shah ("mountain of light!"). And Koh-i-noor is the name by which the diamond has been known ever since. But Nadir Shah was not to enjoy it for long. He was murdered by one of his own courtiers, and possession of the Koh-i-noor passed through a succession of satanic sultans and swashbuckling adventurers, always accompanied by imaginative forms of mayhem. One owner, for example, was encouraged (unsuccessfully) to disclose the gem's hiding place by means of a circular plaster container that was placed around his head and filled with boiling oil. Another proprietor was blinded and imprisoned by his own brother, who was in turn blinded and exiled by yet another brother, all for ownership of the Koh-i-noor.

By 1813, the gem was back in India, this time in the hands of one Ranjit Singh, otherwise known as the Lion of the Punjab, who had waged war to obtain it and who kept it until his death in 1839. Ten years later, after annexing the Punjab region, British authorities found the Koh-i-noor in the city treasury of Lahore. They confiscated the stone (and everything else they found in the strong room) to pay for the expenses of fighting an army of Sikhs who had disputed the British concept of empire.

But the drama of the Koh-i-noor was not yet over. Sent to London as a gift for Queen Victoria, it was received with distinct disappointment because of its crude faceting and dullish look. In 1852 the Royal Family decided to have it recut in the hope of displaying more inner fire.

The delicate operation was carried out with all the ceremonial care that might have attended the birth of a royal infant. Under the guidance of the crown jewelers, Queen Victoria decided on the stone's new shape and style; a four-horsepower steam engine was assembled; Prince Albert set the gem in the dop, or hold, in which it was to be ground; the Duke of Wellington started the engine; and an expert Amsterdam diamond cutter whose name has been recorded only as Voorsanger set about his delicate task.

Voorsanger devoted 38 twelve-hour days to the operation, among other things reducing the gem from 187 to 108.93 carats. But when he was finished, the Koh-i-noor seemed no more brilliant than before. It was relegated to a box in Windsor Castle for 59 years, then placed in the crown worn by Queen Mary at her coronation in 1911 and finally transferred to another crown. Elizabeth, the present Queen Mother, occasionally wears the jewel as a brooch on ceremonial occasions.

The Mines Where Time Stands Still

Gemstones have seldom been found in greater variety and abundance than in Sri Lanka, the jewel-like island off the tip of India that until 1972 was known as Ceylon. Through the ages, the island's widespread deposits of alluvium, washed down from interior mountains by monsoon rains, have been a legendary source of wealth.

The Macedonian general Nearchus was referring to Sri Lanka when he wrote of an island to the east famed for its translucent gems, and King Solomon is said to have sent there for rare stones with which to woo the Queen of Sheba. Many years later, the 17th Century French traveler Jean Baptiste Tavernier described a river rich in rubies, "which descends from certain high mountains in the middle of the island," and Portuguese and Dutch sailors of his era returned home from Ceylon carrying pouches full of rubies, sapphires, garnets and moonstones.

Sri Lanka remains a seemingly inexhaustible source of at least a dozen kinds of gemstones, from alexandrite to zircon. And the primitive methods by which the gems are mined are almost unchanged from those described by Tavernier. In river shallows, workers in loincloths use long-handled scrapers to rake the bottom for gem-bearing gravel. More often, the gems are concentrated a short distance underground in a layer of sand and gravel called *illam,* and pits up to 50 feet deep must be dug to reach them. The gem gravel is lifted to the surface by hand or by rope winches, and is washed in nearby water holes.

The rough stones are then cut and polished on simple, hand-powered machines by artisans whose sense of touch and timing has been passed down, from master to apprentice, through dozens of generations.

At the foot of Sri Lanka's lushly forested mountains, piles of sandy gravel mark the edge of a small pit where gemstones are mined much as they have been for centuries.

Deepening a gemstone pit in Sri Lanka, a young miner scoops
muddy soil into a basket, which will be passed from hand to hand up
to the surface. The walls of the pit are reinforced with a framework
of sturdy timbers to keep them from collapsing.

Sri Lankan workers stand waist-deep in muddy water to cleanse gemstone-bearing gravel in round baskets called *watti*. Each swirl of the basket washes away sand, clay and pebbles, leaving a residue of heavier stones that is then turned over to a sorter.

In Sri Lanka, crude machines like the one above are still used to transform unremarkable pebbles like the palmful shown below into shining gems. The cutter presses the rough stone against a wheel coated with an abrasive paste made from carborundum and rice husks. With his other hand, he slides a slip-roped stick back and forth, like a violinist with a bow, to operate the wheel. The result, like the piece of quartz at right, may require further cutting after export.

Yet for all its sequestered status, the Koh-i-noor remains one of the most celebrated of all jewels — mute testimony to the fact that, in gemstones, a tempestuous history may be more important than physical perfection. Such histories have surrounded many gemstones with superstitions that embody humanity's darkest fears and fondest hopes. Thus, the tradition that Roman Catholic cardinals wear blue sapphires in their rings had its origin in the medieval belief that that particular stone imparted purity, just as the purple amethyst brought sobriety and the emerald tranquillity. Similarly, some Burmese believe that a ruby, when embedded in the flesh, will ward off bodily harm (excepting, of course, the wound required to put it in place), and the notion that the star sapphire is an effective amulet against witchcraft is by no means extinct among the Singhalese of Sri Lanka. Curiously, the common modern custom of wearing birthstone rings for good luck is relatively recent, probably originating in 18th Century Poland.

Gemstones have also been widely used over the centuries as medicines. Sapphire has been thought to be a cure for eye disease, ruby a remedy for spleen and liver disorders, amethyst an antidote for snakebite (when used in a pendant suspended on a dog-hair cord) and moonstone an aid against consumption. The versatile emerald has been used both as a laxative and as a palliative for dysentery.

During the Middle Ages, when the Black Death ravaged Europe, those who could afford to do so draped themselves in gems of every description in the pathetic belief that the purity of the crystals would save them from the loathsome disease. And then there was the sad case of Pope Clement VII. In 1534, as he lay dying, physicians decided to treat him with powders made of crushed gemstones, including diamonds. During his final fortnight the doctors gorged the poor pontiff with doses worth an estimated 40,000 ducats — whereupon, mercifully, he died.

Among individual gems, perhaps none has attracted such persistent superstition as the extraordinary diamond that once, according to legend, served as an eye in a statue of the Hindu goddess Sita. When the stone was stolen by a Brahman priest, the angry goddess is said to have decreed that bad luck would befall anyone who thereafter wore her eye as jewelry. Jean Baptiste Tavernier acquired the 112-carat diamond in southwest India in 1642, but he evidently got rid of it before Sita's curse could take effect, selling it to France's King Louis XIV. Louis named it the Blue Diamond of the Crown and had it recut into a 67.5-carat stone of teardrop shape. The King himself, it is said, wore the accursed crystal only once, whereupon he contracted a fatal case of smallpox.

The self-styled Sun King's successor, Louis XV, prudently refrained from adorning himself with the French Blue, as it was by then known, but both Louis XVI and his queen, Marie Antoinette, used the diamond and subsequently lost their heads at the hands of revolutionaries.

In 1792, as the French Revolution reached its climax, the gem was stolen from the Royal Treasury and disappeared for 38 years. Then, in 1830, a diamond appeared on the London market that was later identified by its steel blue color as the missing French Blue, now recut into a 44.5-carat crystal. It was bought for $90,000 by Henry Thomas Hope, a British banker and gem collector by whose name the diamond was known thereafter.

There is no evidence that Hope suffered any notable misfortune before his death of natural causes in 1839. But in 1890 the diamond was inherited by

Francis Hope, the Duke of Newcastle. Subsequently, Lord Hope's wife, an American actress, ran away with another man, and the nobleman was later forced to sell the diamond in an unsuccessful attempt to stave off bankruptcy. His unfaithful wife, who had frequently worn the gem, died impoverished in Boston in the early 1940s.

Moving from owner to unfortunate owner, the Hope diamond was credited with a heavy toll in the decades after it left the hands of Lord Hope. An Eastern European prince gave it to his love of the moment, a Folies Bergère dancer, but soon became consumed by jealousy and shot her to death. A Greek gem dealer, soon after selling the Hope, drove off a cliff and was killed, along with his wife and child. The man to whom he had sold the stone, a Turkish sultan named Abdul-Hamid II, possessed it for only a few months before being ousted from power by insurgent Army officers.

In 1911 the Hope diamond was purchased for $154,000 by Evalyn Walsh McLean, the daughter of a gold miner who had struck it rich in Colorado; the beauteous Evalyn had subsequently married the owner of *The Washington Post* and was wealthy enough to indulge her every whim. Although she scoffed at the diamond's curse, she lived to see a son killed in an automobile accident, a daughter dead of an overdose of sleeping pills and her husband confined to a mental institution. Despite such afflictions, Mrs. McLean often wore the diamond, mounted in a necklace with 62 white diamonds, even to casual social affairs. She died in 1947, lonely and slightly dotty, at the age of 61.

After purchasing the Hope from the McLean estate, New York jeweler Harry Winston donated it to the Smithsonian Institution, where it now rests peaceably in the company of a host of other royal gemstones.

Throughout history, gemstones have been a hallmark of majesty, not as mere baubles but as status symbols and as commodities easily convertible into cash during periods of royal crisis. It is thus ironic that the particular set of gems that has been most notoriously associated with royalty never, in fact, came into sovereign hands. Instead, in what has become celebrated as the affair of the Queen's Necklace, France's King Louis XVI and his frivolous Marie Antoinette were the hapless victims of an astounding hoax — one whose pernicious effects helped to hasten their appointments with the guillotine.

The complex intrigue began innocently enough during the reign of Louis XV when the crown jewelers, Charles-Auguste Boehmer and Paul Bassenge, decided to assemble a diamond necklace such as the world had never seen. The King, they felt confident, would be only too eager to purchase the necklace for his greedy mistress, Madame Du Barry.

With this entrepreneurial purpose in mind, the jewelers spent several years in acquiring some of the world's finest diamonds and in designing and stringing their masterpiece. To finance the enterprise, they went deeply into debt, even mortgaging their homes and offices. Then, in 1774, just as the project was nearing completion, calamity struck with the sudden death of the King.

That tragedy left Boehmer and Bassenge with a magnificent necklace of 647 meticulously matched diamonds of the first water — and no buyer. Naturally, the jewelers next focused their hopes on the 24-year-old Louis XVI and his 23-year-old queen. Dazzled by the necklace, Louis was deter-

The flawless Hope diamond, encircled by 16 white diamonds, is one of the world's most celebrated jewels, both for its steel blue beauty and for the dark legends that fill its history.

mined to buy it as a gift for Marie Antoinette, who had just given birth. It seemed a natural gift for a lady whose extravagance and indiscretions had become the talk of the Continent. But with a display of prudence that seems out of character, the Queen turned down the necklace, suggesting (or so her sympathizers later insisted) that Louis would be wiser to spend his money on a new warship.

For years, Boehmer and Bassenge worked unceasingly to persuade Marie Antoinette to change her mind. On one occasion, Boehmer fell weeping to his knees before the Queen. "Madame," he cried, "I am ruined, bankrupt, dishonored if you persist in refusing my necklace. I shall go direct from here and throw myself in the river." When Marie Antoinette seemed to approve of that idea, Boehmer backed away from his threat. The necklace remained unsold.

It was, then, understandable that the desperate jewelers should be overjoyed to receive a promising letter, in 1785, from one Jeanne de Saint-Rémy de Valois de La Motte, who had only recently arrived on the Parisian scene but was already rumored to be a confidante of the Queen's. Madame de La Motte advised them that a *grand seigneur* of the realm was interested in buying their necklace and would shortly call upon the jewelers.

In fact, the young and shapely Madame de La Motte was about to execute a bold and carefully contrived swindle of historic proportions. The orphaned daughter of a profligate baron who had been reduced to stealing vegetables before his death in a Paris poorhouse, Jeanne had developed a steely sense of survival while begging on the streets of Paris and, later, as an unwilling student at a boarding school in Passy. She was, in the words of one court observer, "an ambitious and utterly unprincipled woman who would stop at nothing to achieve her ends; thrown into a crowd of elegant toadies, scalawags, schemers and hangers-on, she proved herself a star in the Versailles school of vice."

The *grand seigneur* she had arranged to introduce to the crown jewelers was a prince of the realm and a cardinal of the church, Louis René Édouard de Rohan, who had fallen out of favor with Marie Antoinette and was desperately seeking reinstatement. The comely Jeanne, apparently with the enthusiastic approval of her scoundrel husband, had seduced the cardinal, and in more ways than one. While sharing his bed she had been working to convince him that she was an intimate of the Queen's and was capable of engineering his return to royal grace.

She clinched her argument, and sealed his fate, with a ploy of incredible audacity. Touring the underworld of Paris with her husband, she found a prostitute who bore some physical resemblance to Marie Antoinette and hired her to "do a small service for the Queen." The woman agreed to accompany the de La Mottes to Versailles, to wear a dress they would provide and to station herself in a park beyond the palace with her face veiled. Thus accoutered, she would await the arrival of "a very grand seigneur" — none other than Cardinal de Rohan, who had been transported by joy when Jeanne told him that Marie Antoinette had agreed to a secret tryst under cover of darkness.

The confrontation took only a few moments. The bogus queen simply handed Rohan a rose with the enigmatic words: "You know what that means." Then, as the prince-cardinal flung himself at her feet, she scurried away into the night.

Thus, when Jeanne de La Motte later asked him to act as the Queen's negotiator in purchasing the fabulous necklace of Mssrs. Boehmer and Bassenge, the bedazzled Rohan eagerly agreed.

And the cardinal proved a shrewd bargainer, persuading the jewelers not only to lower their price somewhat, to 1,600,000 francs, but to turn over the necklace to him a full six months before the first installment was due. In turn, the cardinal promptly gave the diamond strands to Madame de La Motte for delivery — or so he thought — to his beloved Marie Antoinette.

Jeanne and her husband wasted not a moment in dismantling the necklace and splitting the loot. While he wisely departed for London, Jeanne, with typical recklessness, remained in Paris. She had some of the diamonds set into bracelets, pendants and rings for her own use; with the proceeds from others, she bought costly clothes and expensive furnishings for a new house, took to collecting high-priced mechanical toys and began riding about town in a coach ornate enough for royalty.

Meanwhile, Cardinal de Rohan was waiting anxiously and in vain for Marie Antoinette to display some public sign of her gratitude. More to the point, the crown jewelers soon wanted their money. Finally, despite Jeanne de La Motte's best efforts to delay the day of reckoning, Boehmer went to Marie Antoinette herself for payment.

The elaborate hoax was immediately exposed, and Louis XVI was moved, as he said later in a letter, to "righteous indignation at such unheard of temerity, such an audacious effort to trade on an august name, and such a daring violation of the respect due to the royal majesty." Although it was well within his power to settle the matter behind closed doors and to exact any penalty he wished, Louis offered Jeanne and the cardinal the opportunity of a public trial.

That was a mistake. Given a platform, Jeanne de La Motte launched a torrent of accusatory lies, insisting throughout the trial that she was the victim of a greedy and ungrateful Queen. Such was the temper of the times

Shaded from the sun, slaves in 18th Century Brazil wash diamond-bearing river gravel under the supervision of inspectors armed with whips. A slave who found an especially large diamond might be rewarded with freedom.

A beautifully cut topaz from Brazil owned by the Smithsonian Institution is prized for its large size, 3,273 carats, and for its striking natural blue color. Most topaz is yellow or colorless.

that she was believed by a multitude of French citizens already seething with dissatisfaction about the corrupt regime and about the Queen, who was already widely known as "the Harlot of Versailles."

Adding fuel to the fire that would one day engulf Marie Antoinette were the words used by Rohan's judges. The cardinal had been accused of the crime of lese majesty for his assumption that the Queen of France would rendezvous with him in the dark thickets of the Versailles gardens. Declared the judges: "We cannot find Cardinal de Rohan guilty of 'criminal presumption' in accepting the idea. With her Most Christian Majesty's reputation for frivolity and indiscretion, with her succession of male and female favorites of dubious repute, we find it entirely plausible that Cardinal de Rohan would do so."

For her part, Jeanne de La Motte was sentenced to be "flogged and beaten, naked, with rods," to be branded by a hot iron applied to the shoulder with the letter V (for *voleuse,* or thief) and to spend the rest of her days as an inmate of the female house of correction at Salpêtrière. But within a year, unknown sympathizers helped Jeanne de La Motte escape. She fled to London, where her worthless husband, wishing no more of her wild schemes, shunned her. Four years later, Madame de La Motte died when she fell or, it has been suggested, was flung from the third floor of a London building.

The luckless Louis XVI and Marie Antoinette never recovered from the scandal of which they were the unknowing and helpless victims. And although the Paris mobs would doubtless have eventually surged to the barricades in any event, the pace of insurgency was surely quickened by Jeanne de La Motte's great hoax. Indeed, no less an authority than Honoré Gabriel de Mirabeau, himself a herald of rebellion, called the affair of the Queen's Necklace "the prelude to revolution."

With the possible exception of 22 stones that later turned up in a necklace owned by the Duke of Sutherland, which may or may not have belonged to the Queen's Necklace, the diamonds lovingly assembled by the French crown jewelers were scattered forever. It has been estimated, however, that the spectacular collection would bring at least eight million dollars on the modern market. Such a price is a tribute not merely to the intrinsic value of the gems, but to the stories and legends that surround them. That being the case, it is instructive to consider the status of two gemstone varieties only recently discovered.

In July 1967, a Portuguese prospector named Manuel d'Souza was wandering through the East African bush in Tanzania. "I turned left instead of right," d'Souza subsequently recalled, "and I got lost. I came to a deserted Masai village. Some natives came up and showed me some stones." Unimpressed by what he was offered, d'Souza asked the natives if they could show him anything more interesting. They led him into the jungle, where he found lying loose on the ground some stones whose rich purplish blue color delighted him. He thought they were sapphires, but they turned out to be zoisite, a mineral that had been known for at least a century but always before had been found in a drab green suitable only for ashtrays and other souvenir trifles. But in its beautiful blue form, zoisite is presently being marketed — by the New York firm of Tiffany and Co. among others — as tanzanite, after the country of its origin.

D'Souza's find inevitably attracted other prospectors to East Africa, among them a Scottish geologist, Campbell Bridges. And in 1967, while seeking tanzanite in East Africa, Bridges discovered a deposit of stones whose pure green hue excelled even that of most emeralds. Tiffany named the gemstone, a variety of garnet, tsavorite, in honor of Kenya's Tsavo National Park.

Considering their beauty and rarity, tanzanite and tsavorite should command splendid prices. Yet tanzanite sells for about $\frac{1}{15}$ the price of sapphire, while tsavorite may bring only $500 a carat, against the $6,000 that buyers are willing to pay for emeralds.

Jean Baptiste Tavernier would have understood this apparent discrepancy immediately. He knew that no gemstone becomes truly valuable until it has accumulated a rich history. Ω

THE INNER WORLD OF GEMSTONES

For all their external splendor, many gemstones also enclose magnificence on a smaller scale, in the form of tiny bits of foreign matter, fissures or irregularities in their crystalline structures. The Roman naturalist Pliny the Elder effused that the vistas within a gem "proclaim the majesty of Nature." To the gemologists of today, the spectacles revealed by microscopic examination offer more specific kinds of information: clues to the nature of the geologic processes that form and shape gems.

Most gemstones crystallize within the earth's crust in pockets of magma or vapor, or in high-temperature solutions of elements and water. Frequently, a growing crystal engulfs some of its environment, trapping another crystal or a pocket of liquid or gas and preserving it for the ages. Even if a gemstone remains pure, it may accrete layers of crystal material that differ in color; internal stresses may build up during rapid growth and cause a crystal to crack, or separate crystals may grow together in a single interlinked mass.

Once formed, a gem remains vulnerable to other processes that can mark it indelibly: Caustic substances may etch it, geologic upheaval may crack it, or, as a gem cools after its formation, atoms of a foreign substance distributed throughout the crystal may congregate to form an internal array of crystals.

Such minute manifestations of gemstone history — some of them shown here and on the following pages, with the photographic magnification specified in each case — can be invaluable to gemological detective work. The tiny crystals of other minerals enveloped in Colombian emeralds vary so distinctively from site to site that they indicate the very mine an emerald comes from. And the microscopic inclusions found in some diamond crystals present geologists with a valuable gift they can get no other way — a tiny sample of the material to be found in the impossibly remote, molten depths of the earth.

DIAMOND (200×)
Triangular marks left in the outermost layers of a diamond when crystal growth halted pock the face of the uncut gem. The technique used to photograph the diamond highlighted the surface contours with streaks of color.

Minute Evidence of Crystal Growth

Natural crystals, the products of geologic turmoil, rarely form a perfect gemstone. Under the microscope, a seemingly flawless gem may display evidence of a turbulent history of uneven or disrupted crystal growth.

Some gemstones exhibit a pattern of concentric bands — the mineralogical equivalent of a tree's growth rings — caused by an irregular flow of crystal-forming magma or solution into the underground chamber that harbored the developing gemstone. The banding is especially vivid in certain colored gems, where each successive influx of fluid that contributed crystal material to the gem's growth contained a slightly different proportion of pigment.

Another kind of layering can be found in some rubies and sapphires that in ordinary light may appear to consist of a single perfect crystal. When viewed under polarized light, these gems can be seen to consist of numerous separate, wafer-like layers.

Disruptions in crystal growth often add distinctive signatures to the composition of a gem. When a solid — usually a tiny crystal of another substance — settles on a face of a developing crystal, it can hinder or completely block a small area of growth. As the crystal continues to build on all sides, a disturbance, visible as a change in color or even as a slender, elongated cavity, appears in the growth pattern, oriented in the precise direction of crystal growth.

Another flaw related to the geometry of crystal formation may appear after crystal growth is complete. Under intense heat and pressure, corrosive solutions sometimes eat into a gem. The resulting corrosion trails invariably follow the lines of the gem's fundamental crystalline framework.

TSAVORITE (25×)
A threadlike pattern of corrosion etches
the interior of a tsavorite. The scars (which
are distorted by an optical effect of the
gem's faceted surface) were caused by a corrosive
solution that attacked the gemstone along
lines of weakness in its crystalline structure.

RUBY (25×)
Multiple crystals pattern a ruby, photographed in polarized light, with distinct zones of color. The varying shades result from the interaction of the polarized light with the differently oriented planes of interlocked atoms in each separate crystal layer.

SAPPHIRE (40×)
A tiny particle on the surface of a growing sapphire created a visible trail of disturbed crystalline material as the gemstone engulfed it and continued to grow. The gem's banded coloration records changes in the composition of the solution in which it formed.

The Telltale Inclusions

Transparent gems often showcase other tiny crystals — relics of their mineralogical origins — in their brilliant depths. In some instances, crystals of different substances may have grown side by side in the same solution or pocket of magma until one, the future gem, outstripped and overgrew its neighbor.

Inclusions generated by this process can sometimes be recognized by their sharp angles and unmarred facets, preserved since their formation within the rocky armor of another crystal. The chipped and abraded appearance of an inclusion, on the other hand, may betray its greater age with scars that could only have been acquired over the course of many millions of years, before the newer crystal host engulfed the tiny guest.

Some enclosed crystals actually took shape after the gemstone was complete. At the high temperatures and pressures of gem formation, substances that are usually incompatible can coexist in a single crystalline lattice; but as conditions moderate after crystal formation, the less abundant substance may separate again into distinct crystals, arrayed throughout the host crystal and oriented in accordance with its crystalline planes.

Such inclusions of other minerals are among the surest indicators of a gemstone's provenance: Each gem-bearing region is marked by a distinctive array of minerals that surrounded and infiltrated its developing gemstones.

DIAMOND (10×)
The ghostly outline of a tiny eight-sided diamond crystal is visible beneath the faceted surface of a larger diamond. The smaller crystal, probably much older than its host, may have acted as the seed around which the larger gemstone took shape.

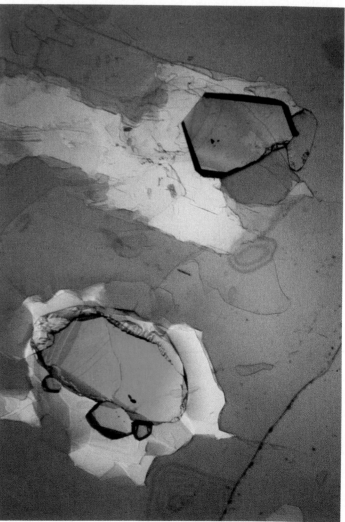

TOPAZ (65×)
Suffused in polarized light, tiny crystals of clear quartz appear green, while the surrounding matrix of yellow topaz glows violet. The quartz and topaz crystals probably interlocked as fluids that contained both minerals began to crystallize.

SAPPHIRE (40×)
Glinting from the depths of a pink sapphire, a tiny prism of the mineral apatite probably crystallized at the same time as the gem, but the apatite prism grew more slowly and was engulfed.

EMERALD (40×)
A mass of brassy pyrite hovers in the interior of an emerald. Inclusions of pyrite, formed simultaneously with their hosts, are the hallmark of emeralds from Colombia's Chivor mine.

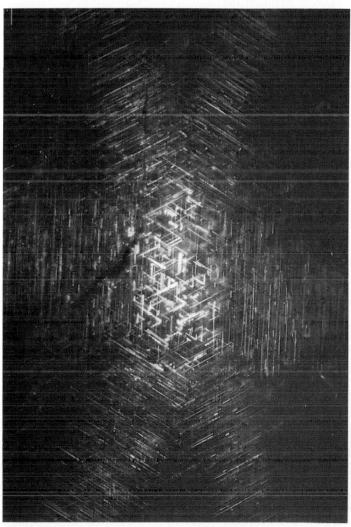

RUBY (30×)
Tiny spangles of the mineral rutile arrayed inside a star ruby reflect the six-rayed glow that earns the gem its name. Dispersed molecules of rutile coalesced after the ruby took shape, forming needle-like crystals that parallel the gem's crystalline planes.

SAPPHIRE (45×)
Snowy crystals of feldspar, embedded in a sapphire that came from Thailand, crystallized within the parent rock, basalt, at the same time as the gemstone was being formed. Inclusions of feldspar are characteristic of Thailand's sapphires.

Traces of a Liquid Past

Crystals that solidified in a vein of cooling magma bear no trace of their liquid origin. But gemstones that took shape in a mineral-rich water solution often enclose minuscule liquid mementos of their genesis.

Fissures, which frequently open during rapid crystal growth, can fill with the solution in which the gemstone is developing; new crystal material can then solidify in the fracture, sealing in stray drops of liquid. Entombed in the crack, the droplets reveal themselves, when viewed microscopically, by their iridescent colors — a product of the same optical effect, called interference, that imparts color to a thin film of oil.

Larger voids sometimes are left within the crystal structure; the growing crystal may block the circulation of the feed solution, for example, leaving a portion of the crystal starved for new deposits of mineral. As the rest of the crystal grows apace, a hollow develops. Then, if the solution begins once again to flow to the starved area, the cavity may be roofed over with crystallized material, trapping a droplet of fluid.

Often, these larger inclusions of liquid also contain particles of solid and bubbles of gas — further evidence of the rich mineralogical brews in which the gems were spawned.

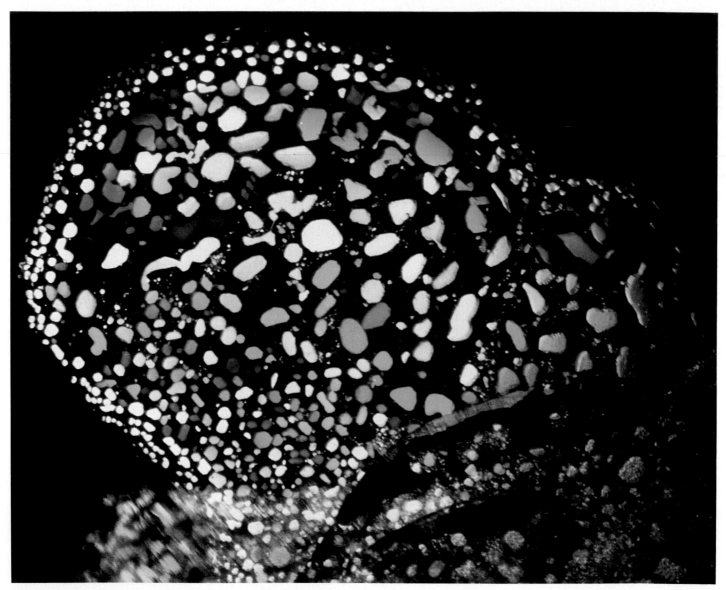

BERYL (50×)
A mosaic of color marks tiny regions of fluid that have been trapped along a fracture in beryl. White light reflecting from the thin layers of liquid has been transformed into spatters of color by an optical phenomenon called interference.

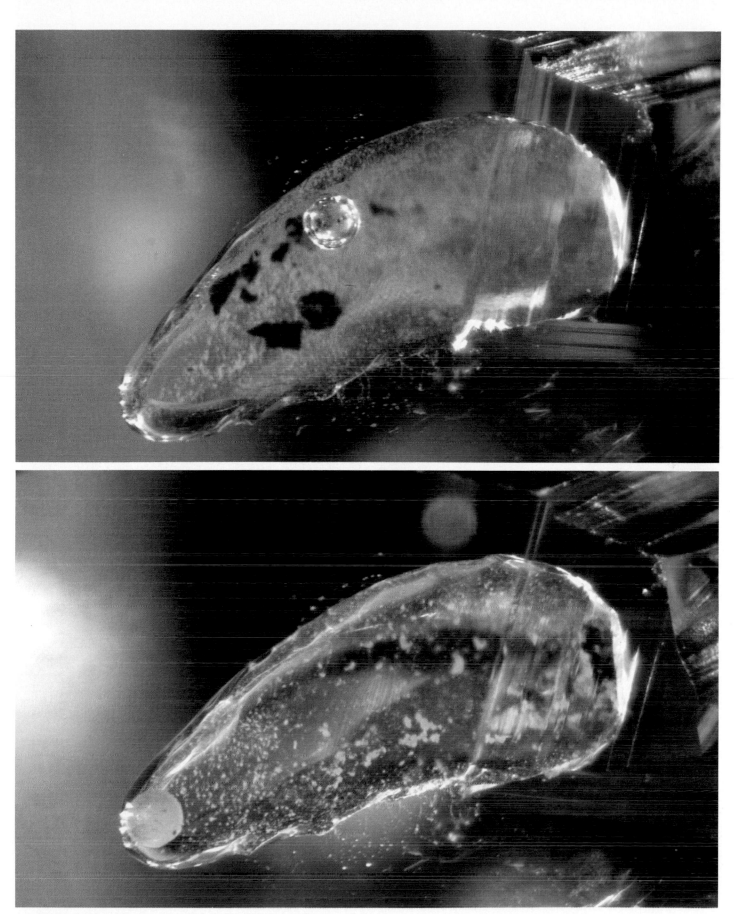

QUARTZ (40×)
A cavity in a quartz crystal encloses a microcosm of gas, mineral-rich water, and flecks of yellow and black minerals *(top)*. When the quartz is agitated, the gas bubble tumbles through the fluid, capturing flecks of the yellow solid *(above)*.

The Unexpected Beauty of Flaws

Perhaps the richest sources of microscopic splendor within gemstones are the various cracks that occur during a gem's formation and throughout its subsequent history. As a crystal grows, internal stresses build up that eventually may cause it to crack; rapid growth makes a crystal especially vulnerable. An influx of crystal-forming solution may deposit enough mineral within the crack to heal it. But often the fracture is left only partly filled, enlivened with exquisite patterns of feathers and filigrees that were created as the tenuous deposits of crystal material aligned in accordance with the rigid geometry of crystal growth. When they are properly illuminated, such partially healed fractures often shimmer in vivid colors, created by optical interference.

A fully formed gemstone buried in the earth's crust is subject to stress from such geologic upheavals as mountain building, volcanism and earthquakes. All can strain the gem enough to fracture it — and because the solutions necessary for crystal growth are no longer present, such cracks remain unhealed. The result is the paradoxical product of gem flaws — minute beauty.

SAPPHIRE (45×)
Zoned with rainbow colors, fractures halo dark inclusions of liquid in sapphire. When this gem was exposed to intense heat in the laboratory — duplicating conditions that occur deep in the earth — the liquid expanded and shattered the surrounding crystal.

BERYL (55×)
The scalloped contours of a flaw in beryl typify the shell-shaped, or conchoidal, fractures that result when a gemstone is split across its crystalline planes. These irregular breaks contrast with the clean and regular cleavage that occurs along the crystal's lines of weakness.

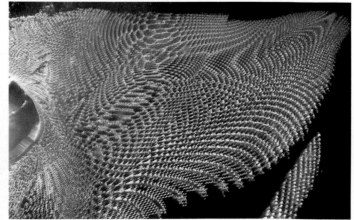

QUARTZ (80×)
A quartz crystal that split during its formation is webbed with silvery channels of liquid or gas, which were woven into a strikingly regular pattern by intervening deposits of quartz that formed within the crack as the crystal continued to grow.

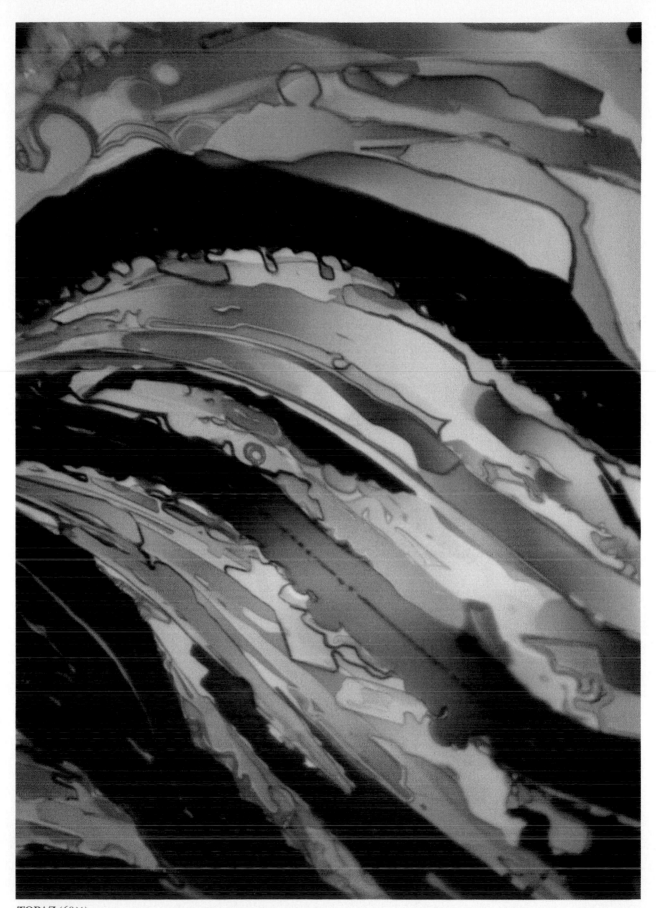

TOPAZ (60×)
Richly colored bands glow within a flaw in topaz as light reflects from
the cleavage. An optical effect called interference lends rainbow
colors to the streaks of gas in the imperfection. The dark zones are
regions where deposits of crystal material healed the flaw.

EARTH'S CRUCIBLES OF CREATION

Pedro the Cruel, a 14th Century Spanish king, was by any criterion a cad. He abandoned one wife after two days of marriage, another after three, murdered numerous priests and noblemen (including his own brother) and in general disported himself in such a manner as to push his subjects into rebellion. Driven from his own country, Pedro fled to Bordeaux, in France, where the formidable English warrior Edward, the Black Prince, was holding court. Pedro enlisted Edward's aid in a campaign to regain his throne, promising as payment a considerable treasure in money and land.

At the Battle of Nájera in 1367, Edward duly defeated a force led by one Sancho the Stammerer and returned the wicked king to his throne. For his pains, Edward received from Pedro a single two-inch-long red gem — which to this day resides as the centerpiece of the British Crown of State and is renowned as the Black Prince's ruby.

Only after the passage of centuries was it discovered that the Black Prince's ruby is not a ruby at all. It is, alas, a chunk of spinel, a mineral sometimes mistaken for ruby — but worth only a fraction as much.

The gemstone family abounds in such look-alikes. Certain red garnets, for example, are sometimes sold as "Cape rubies" or "Arizona rubies." Citrine, a variety of the world's most common mineral, quartz, can be mistaken for yellow topaz — which in turn can resemble yellow sapphire. Much of the diamond's majesty can be imparted to the drab, brownish zircon by the careful application of heat. And, with advances in technology, an expert's knowledge is required to tell the difference between some sophisticated synthetic and imitation gems and the real thing.

Identification is thus a major mission of gemology, a science that leads its practitioners down many mysterious paths. It begins with speculations about the utterly inaccessible regions of enormous heat and pressure that lie more than 100 miles below the surface of the earth. (The deepest penetration yet achieved by humans — a research shaft being drilled by Soviet scientists on the Kola Peninsula, east of Finland — has so far reached a depth of only six miles.) Gemologists also inquire into the origins and nature of the basic rock types in which gemstones are found, analyze the chemical makeup and atomic arrangements of crystals, and study the behavior of light and such gem properties as hardness, refractive index and specific gravity.

All of these factors contribute to the differences between gemstones and more plebeian materials. Except for such gem substances as pearl, amber, coral and ivory — which originate in living things — all gems are minerals. But they are set apart from minerals such as mica, calcite and gypsum by

A beam of light passing through a plastic model shows why a badly cut diamond lacks sparkle: Light entering the top facet *(left)* reflects from one side and leaks out the other. In a properly proportioned diamond, light strikes both lower facets at a shallow angle, is reflected each time and flashes back toward its source through the top of the gem.

their rarity, durability and beauty. In some gemstones, only one or two of these qualities predominate. Other gems, such as diamonds, possess all three in abundance, and hence are invariably the most prized.

The fascination with beautiful stones since the beginning of civilization has produced numerous theories of their origins — including the intriguing idea that they reproduce themselves sexually. Scientific investigation has dispelled most of the myths, and it is now generally understood that mineral gemstones are formed in extraordinary circumstances within and below the crust of the earth.

The necessary conditions vary widely from one kind of gem to another, but nearly all involve certain constituent elements of the earth combining in exactly the right proportions, being subjected to immense forces of heat and pressure, then cooling and solidifying at particular rates for just the right amounts of time. The odds against the incidence of these combinations of conditions are enormous — hence, the relative rarity of precious gems.

While some principles of gemstone formation can be deduced with a high degree of probability, myriad tantalizing details remain unexplained. For example, no gem has been more closely studied than the diamond — and none has proved more unwilling to reveal the secrets of its conception.

In its origins, the diamond — a crystalline form of pure carbon — is doubtless the most deep-seated of all gemstones: Almost certainly, the process of its creation begins 90 to 120 miles beneath the surface of the planet in the upper part of the earth's mantle, the 1,800-mile-thick region that lies between the molten outer core and the solid, rocky crust. The upper mantle is thought to consist of heavy iron- and magnesium-rich rocks — particularly dark, coarse-grained peridotite — interspersed in many places with molten rock, called magma.

But geologists agree only on the barest outlines of the processes that create diamonds in these hidden depths and then transport them toward the surface. From laboratory efforts to synthesize diamonds, scientists have concluded that temperatures of at least 2,732° F. and pressures of 975,000 pounds per square inch — 65,000 times the normal atmospheric pressure — are required to cause atoms of carbon to crystallize in this most exalted of its guises. They agree, too, that diamonds reside chiefly in so-called diamond pipes — slender, spike-shaped formations of volcanic rock carried for miles through the earth's crust, from the upper mantle to the surface, by ancient volcanic eruptions.

Beyond these few certainties little is known, although theories abound. One of them has it that carbon, in the form of carbon dioxide, may dissolve in the magma of the mantle. If a series of complex physical and chemical processes somehow produced a saturated solution, excess carbon might crystallize out in the form of diamonds. But the source of the carbon is a puzzle, for the mantle contains only a tiny proportion of so-called juvenile carbon — carbon that is part of the primal stuff of the earth. Living organisms produce carbon in the form of proteins, carbohydrates and other organic substances, and some scientists think these organic processes might be the source of the diamond-forming carbon. It got to the mantle, they theorize, when once-living matter, such as coal or the skeletons of tiny marine animals that make up deposits of limestone and chalk, was plowed under the earth's surface into the mantle by the movement of the enormous

The two-inch lump of red spinel known erroneously as the Black Prince's ruby glows amid other splendid stones on the British Crown of State. Red spinel often passed for ruby before the development of analytical techniques capable of distinguishing between the two gems.

plates of crustal material described by the theory of plate tectonics. In places where adjacent plates are inching toward each other, one may plunge beneath the other; called subduction, this is one of the many tectonic processes that continually alter the face of the earth.

Scientists are not sure where in the upper mantle diamonds were formed. Some believe that diamonds crystallized in the same magma that later carried them up the diamond pipes. But others dispute that notion, claiming that the upwelling material merely acted as a geological conveyor belt, sweeping along lumps of diamond-bearing rock formed elsewhere in the mantle. However the process worked, it would seem to be over; no new diamond pipe has formed in the past 15 million years or so.

For all the mysteries attending the creation of diamonds, their source on the earth's surface is well known: deposits of a rock called kimberlite, named after the South African town of Kimberley, where it was identified in 1880. Once described as "a geological plum pudding," kimberlite is the heterogeneous product of a chaotic history, for it is the rock that was blasted upward from the mantle through diamond pipes. Besides solidified magma of various kinds, it contains bits of rock swept along on its violent journey, and exhibits the effects of oxidation and exposure to groundwater.

Identified in Africa, Brazil, India, Australia, North America and Siberia, diamond-bearing kimberlite deposits are found only in the oldest and most stable continental regions, far from the tumultuous zones where the rigid plates that make up the earth's crust draw apart, grind past one another or collide. The crust is thickest beneath these ancient, undisturbed continental shields, and its weight creates pressures high enough to form diamond at the top of the mantle — the zone from which kimberlite deposits erupted.

The precise nature of the titanic forces that thrust kimberlite magma through perhaps 25 miles of overlying crust is not known. But geologists believe that high-pressure pockets of superheated gases such as steam and carbon dioxide are the most likely source of the impetus. As the magma shot upward in slender columns, it may have exploited zones of weakness in the bedrock created by the stresses of tectonic processes occurring elsewhere: Many kimberlite deposits date from the period between 70 and 150 million years ago when ponderous crustal motions were splitting a single great land mass into the separate continents of South America and Africa (although kimberlite deposits as much as 1.2 billion years old have been found).

Once the magma found a route, its ascent was swift — perhaps a matter of a few hours — and the eruption of the kimberlite at the surface was a cataclysmic volcanic event. Because it probably contained a large proportion of solid rock, both from the mantle and from the intermediate layers of bedrock, the kimberlite did not spurt from surface fissures as fluid lava does, although the eruption may have rained ash and rock fragments on the surrounding terrain. Instead, the pressure of the ascending magma probably caused the surface rock to bulge upward, then collapse at the center as the gases that drove the kimberlite were released. In the resulting crater, the kimberlite hardened into a deposit of rock from a few hundred yards to a mile wide. Finding such deposits today is far from easy because eons of erosion have planed down the surrounding bulge of rock. And when found, the deposit may not contain diamonds; only one out of every 200 kimberlite deposits in South Africa is worth mining.

Kimberlite is an igneous rock — that is, a rock formed of magma which

has cooled in the depths of the earth or has spilled onto the surface as lava, then solidified. And igneous rock is a rich source of many prized gems besides diamonds. As magma wells up into underground fissures or magma chambers and cools, most of it hardens into prosaic rock such as granite. But in the nether reaches of a magma pocket, trace elements in the molten rock may become concentrated, producing magma that is rich in water, dissolved gases and rare elements. In such cases the water slows the process of solidification, allowing large crystals to grow from the concentrations of elements. The crystal-laced deposit that results is known as a pegmatite, and, depending on the composition of the original magma, it may contain such gems as topaz, tourmaline, aquamarine and garnet.

Like every other form of rock on the earth's surface, igneous rock breaks down when assailed by water, wind, ice or chemicals in the atmosphere. Gravity, wind and moving water conspire to sweep away the fragments and redeposit them as sediment on riverbeds, alluvial plains and the floors of seas. Under the weight of succeeding layers of detritus, the debris is compacted and cemented to form the second of the earth's three major kinds of rock: sedimentary rock, which includes sandstone, shale and limestone.

Most gems in sedimentary rock did not originate there, but were transported from deposits elsewhere, perhaps great distances away. When the slow processes of erosion break down rock, the harder gem minerals remain intact and are washed slowly downstream. If the gemstones are chemically inert and hard enough to resist long periods of rolling and tumbling, they work their way downward in stream beds and gradually collect in what are known as placer deposits. A few gemstones, such as turquoise and opal, actually form in sedimentary rock. Groundwater seeping downward through layers of silica-rich volcanic ash, for instance, may pick up traces of the silica, then redeposit it in crevices within the rock as an aggregate of microscopic particles—an opal. Because sedimentary rock frequently entombs plant and animal matter, the opal sometimes finds a home in the interstices of a buried shell, a bone or, most commonly, an ancient log, forming an opalized fossil. Turquoise is the issue of a similar process of seepage and mineral deposition; only the elements involved differ.

Gemstones are also produced in the third kind of terrestrial rock, the metamorphic rock that is formed when volcanic activity, deep burial or the tectonic processes that fold crustal rock and uplift mountains subject igneous and sedimentary rock to enormous heat and pressure, fundamentally changing the character of the rock. In the process, trace minerals distributed throughout the original rock are freed and may concentrate to form deposits of gems. Garnet usually forms in a metamorphic rock called mica schist, which is created by regional metamorphism when extensive layers of igneous and sedimentary rock are transformed by tectonic activity. Similarly, the fabled rubies and sapphires of Burma are the result of contact metamorphism; underground magma was thrust into layers of impure limestone, metamorphosing the limestone into gem-studded marble.

Whatever the manner of their formation, gemstones possess characteristics that are dictated by their chemical ingredients and by the way in which those ingredients are arranged.

All matter on earth is composed of elements—substances that cannot be broken down by chemical means—of which 92 have been identified in the earth's crust. Some, such as the oxygen and hydrogen in the atmosphere and the gold and diamonds that can be sifted from some stream beds, exist in pure form, but most are chemically gregarious and usually exist in combination with other elements as compounds. Although a mere eight elements make up 98.5 per cent of the crust's total weight, they combine, along with much smaller proportions of a few rare elements, into about 3,000 naturally occurring compounds. Collectively, these materials that constitute the earth's crust are known as minerals.

Rigid strictures inherent in the atomic makeup of an element govern how it can link up with other elements. The simple mineral corundum — one variant of which is ruby — is a compound of aluminum and oxygen, with atoms bonded in a ratio of 2 of aluminum to 3 of oxygen, while spinel combines magnesium, aluminum and oxygen in a ratio of 1 to 2 to 4. In addition to the fixed ratios of their constituents, most minerals are also characterized by an unvarying geometric arrangement of the interlinked atoms. Itself invisible, this characteristic atomic geometry gives rise to one of the most notable of gemstone characteristics: their crystalline structure.

The study of crystals — a word that originated as the Greek *krystallos,* which in turn is derived from *kryos,* meaning "icy cold," reflecting the ancient belief that quartz crystal was water permanently frozen into rock — is in itself a science, and a difficult one at that. One of the first scientists to study crystals was Nicolaus Steno, a 17th Century Danish geologist and Catholic priest who formulated a law with the forbidding name of The Constancy of Interfacial Angles. It states that in all crystals of a particular mineral, the angles between corresponding sets of external surfaces, or faces, are always the same. That being the case, crystals of quartz (the mineral used in Steno's experiments) may be microscopic in size or huge, may come in a wide variety of external shapes, and may be found in any part of the world — yet the angles formed by similar pairs of faces are identical.

Steno's discovery hinted at an underlying order in the multitude of crystal shapes, and it was greatly elaborated in the early 19th Century by the Abbé René Just Haüy, professor of minerology at the Museum of Natural History in Paris, honorary canon of the Cathedral of Notre Dame and a scholar with a touch of poesy in his soul. Speaking of the realm of minerals, he called crystals "the flowers of the kingdom."

One day in the late 1700s (or so the story goes), while visiting at the home of a friend, Haüy was examining a specimen of calcite when, to his considerable embarrassment, he dropped it. When he picked up the shattered fragments, he noticed that all of them, large and small, had the same shape. In the thrill of revelation, Haüy shouted *"Tout est trouvé!"* — "All is discovered!" — and dashed back to his laboratory.

There, he set about smashing chunks of calcite. Yet even after he had pulverized the material to sand-sized grains, he found that each tiny piece had the shape of a rhombohedron — a solid with six faces and edges of equal length, like a cube, but distorted so that each face is diamond-shaped. Haüy concluded that if he pulverized calcite into its smallest units, they too would be rhombohedral. And he guessed that crystals of every other mineral are also built up of tiny, indivisible units of a characteristic shape.

To explain the fact that crystals of the same mineral may take several forms despite the internal similarities he had detected, Haüy made an inspired leap. On some crystal faces, he reasoned, the tiny units are arranged not in an even layer but in a pattern of infinitesimal steps, creating a plane that actually cuts across the matrix of tiny crystalline units, in much the same manner as the sloping side of an Egyptian pyramid angles across each of the stepped rectangular blocks of which it is constructed. Because the building blocks are so tiny relative to the whole structure, the stepped pattern is invisible, and the face appears smooth.

Still, the shape of a crystal — declared Haüy — must be related to the shape of its constituent units, no matter how different it appears to be, because there is a limited number of slopes that can cut cleanly across an array of indivisible units. The side of that illustrative pyramid, for example, must slope according to a simple ratio of blocks — two blocks over for each block up, for instance. Haüy codified this notion in what came to be known as Haüy's Law, which provides a method for identifying the basic unit of a crystal from the angles at which its faces cut across imaginary internal axes.

The indivisible units that Haüy detected are in fact tiny, geometrical arrangements of atoms. But it was not until 1912, more than a century after Haüy's pioneering work, that direct evidence was obtained of the atomic basis of crystalline structure. Using a technique called X-ray crystallography, the German physicist Max von Laue aimed beams of X-rays at crystals of various substances and found that, in every case, the rays were deflected by planes of atoms oriented just as Haüy's Law predicted.

This atomic geometry is re-created each time a substance crystallizes. Atoms that dart about erratically, at great speed, in a molten material or in solution begin to coalesce as the melt cools or the solution is concentrated. Drawn together by mutual attractive forces, they arrange themselves in a crystalline latticework with phenomenal rapidity: A crystal may grow at the rate of 16 trillion atoms per hour. It is testimony to the constraints inherent in atomic structure that this process, repeated in the formation of every crystalline gemstone found on earth, always results in the same characteristic crystal shapes *(pages 58-61)*. Natural diamond crystals take the form of a cube, an eight-sided octahedron, or one of several other crystal shapes based on the cube, while emeralds, which belong to the hexagonal crystal system, invariably occur as simple, six-sided prisms.

Just as a crystal system is decreed by the order in which atoms are arranged, so the strength of atomic bonds determines a crystal's hardness — a quality of no small significance in gemstones. Hardness can be most readily defined as the amount of resistance a substance puts up to scratching. For gemstones, existing in a world that is filled with scratchy things, hardness can make the difference between a possession prized for its durable beauty and an attractive but easily marred bauble that has little value as a jewel.

In 1812, a German scientist named Friedrich Mohs devised a rough but handy system that is still used to gauge the hardness of minerals. On a scale of 1 to 10, starting with the softest minerals, he declared that the hardness of talc is 1, gypsum 2, calcite 3, fluorite 4, apatite 5, orthoclase 6, quartz 7, topaz 8, corundum (including ruby and sapphire) 9 and diamond 10.

Thus, gypsum can scratch talc but talc cannot scratch gypsum (the human fingernail, with a hardness of 2.5, can make its mark on both). Emerald, which does not appear on the Mohs scale, can scratch quartz but may itself be scratched by topaz; its hardness obviously falls between the two (it is, in fact, about 7.5).

At 7, the hardness of quartz is especially significant. Quartz is ubiqui-

THE GEOMETRY OF GEMS

The numerous shapes of gem crystals are the outward expression of a precise internal order: a regular, three-dimensional array of the mineral's component atoms. Since the arrangement of atoms depends upon the properties of the elements present, the basic pattern of each mineral's crystalline lattice is distinctive.

To classify these differing arrangements of atoms, crystallographers identify the unit cell — the smallest geometrical pattern of interlinked atoms that is repeated billions of times throughout the crystal. Although the unit cell's components (the number, kinds and ratios of atoms within it) differ with each mineral, only six basic shapes are found

in gem crystals. The shape of the unit cell determines the ultimate shape of the crystal, but even the simplest shape, the cube, or isometric, cell *(right),* gives rise to a multitude of crystal forms known as the isometric system.

In some minerals based on the isometric cell, the faces of the crystals are parallel to the sides of the unit cells and the crystals are themselves cube-shaped. In other, more complex arrangements, the crystal faces cut across the assembly of cubes in a slope that can be described as the result of myriad tiny steps. Because the slope is geometrically related to the unit cell's shape, even the most complex isometric crystals can be identified.

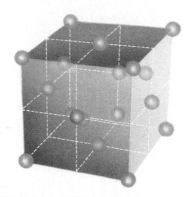

UNIT CELL OF DIAMOND
In a pattern repeated indefinitely throughout a diamond, 18 atoms of carbon link in a minute cube — an isometric cell — that is the basic building block of the stone's crystalline structure.

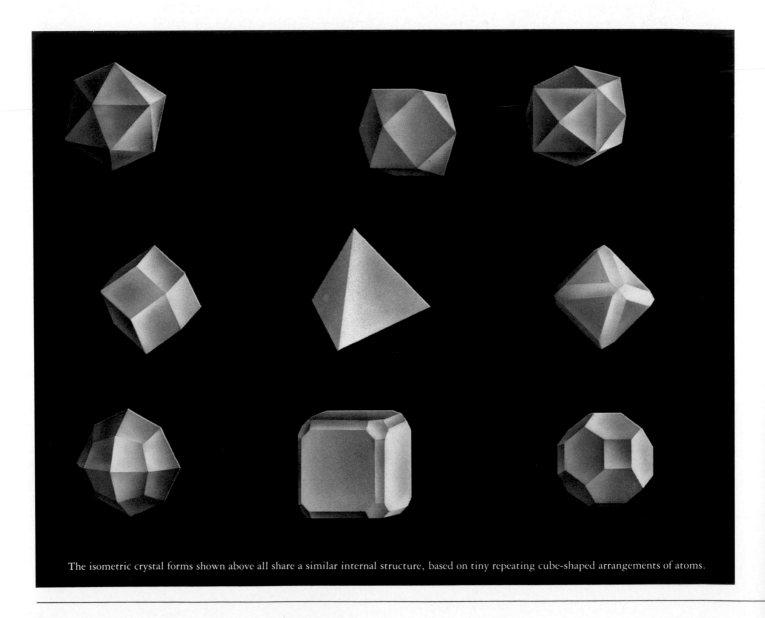

The isometric crystal forms shown above all share a similar internal structure, based on tiny repeating cube-shaped arrangements of atoms.

Massed isometric cells sometimes form cubic crystals. The construction shown schematically above, with the cell's size greatly exaggerated, is typified by the fluorite crystals at right.

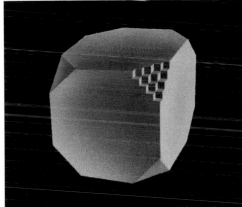

Staggered isometric cells often modify a cube-shaped crystal (*above*). Though their slope is determined by minute steps, the corner faces are smooth, as shown on the fluorite crystal at right.

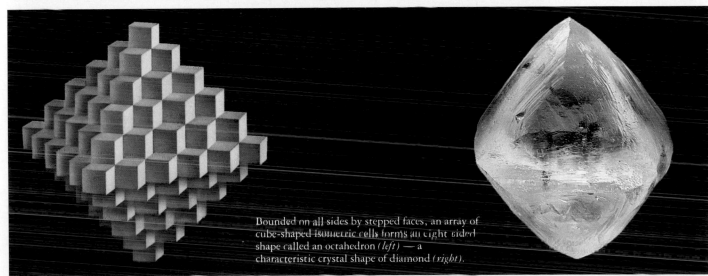

Bounded on all sides by stepped faces, an array of cube-shaped isometric cells forms an eight-sided shape called an octahedron (*left*) — a characteristic crystal shape of diamond (*right*).

The Systems of Crystal Shapes

Among prized gems, only three — diamond, garnet and spinel — are based on the isometric crystal system illustrated on the preceding pages. But each of the five remaining systems also depends on a characteristic shape of unit cell.

The five types of unit cells are distinguished by particular proportions and angles, but all except the hexagonal cell — which gives rise to the crystal family that includes ruby, sapphire and emerald — can be likened to a cube that has been stretched or distorted in one or more directions. These tiny geometrical solids sometimes form crystals that duplicate, on a much larger scale, the shape of their unit cells. But each category also includes more complex crystal shapes, in which the unit cells are arranged stepwise along the crystal faces.

By applying the laws of geometry and crystal growth, mineralogists can identify the unit cell of an unfamiliar crystal from precise measurements of the angles between adjacent faces. But, as shown in the examples on this and the facing page, the general appearance of a crystal sometimes clearly indicates its identity.

THE HEXAGONAL SYSTEM
A unit cell with six identical sides meeting at equal angles *(below)* is the basic structural unit of the hexagonal crystal system. Hexagonal crystals often exhibit a six-sided cross section, as illustrated by the beryl crystal at right.

THE ORTHORHOMBIC SYSTEM
In the unit cell of the orthorhombic system, every pair of intersecting edges forms a right angle, but all three dimensions of the cell differ *(below)*. Orthorhombic crystals, typified by the topaz at right, tend to be boxy in appearance and to display numerous right angles.

THE TETRAGONAL SYSTEM

A unit cell with right-angled corners and two of its three dimensions equal (*below*) is the basic building block of the tetragonal system. A pair of square faces, located on opposite sides of the crystal, sometimes characterizes tetragonal substances, such as wulfenite (*right*).

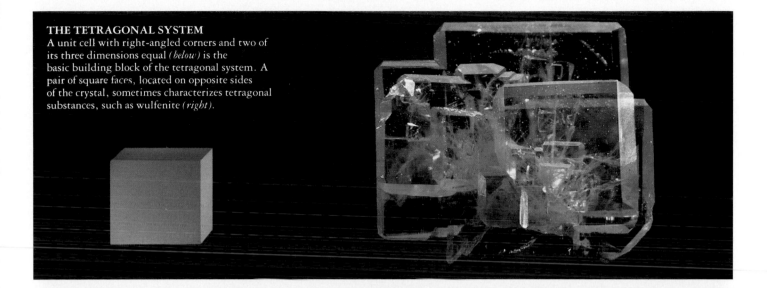

THE MONOCLINIC SYSTEM

All three dimensions of the monoclinic cell differ, and it is skewed in one direction so that, at any corner, only two of the three intersecting edges form a right angle (*below*). Monoclinic crystals, such as sphene (*right*), frequently display both lozenge-shaped and rectangular faces.

THE TRICLINIC SYSTEM

The triclinic cell differs along each of its dimensions, and none of its intersecting edges meet at right angles (*below*). Like their minute constituent cells, triclinic crystals, such as amblygonite (*right*), show no right angles and are asymmetrical in appearance.

tous, appearing as grains of sand, as part of most road-building materials, as filler for coffee sweeteners and even as motes of dust in the air. Wherever and whenever gemstones are worn as human adornments, they inevitably come into contact with quartz particles — and gems with a hardness of less than 7 will eventually suffer disfiguring abrasions.

It is by no means a coincidence that the four most precious gemstones — diamonds, rubies, sapphires and emeralds — are harder than quartz. Conversely, few gemstones softer than quartz are highly sought after as jewels. Among the exceptions — because superficial scratches do not mar the rich colors that are the basis of their appeal — are opal (hardness 5.5 to 6.5) and turquoise (5 to 6), and it is more prudent to display them in pins and pendants than to expose them to the rigorous usage of rings and bracelets.

The intervals between the degrees of hardness that the numbers on the Mohs scale represent are by no means uniform. Indeed, there is less difference between talc (1) and corundum (9) than between corundum and diamond (10) — the hardest of all known substances.

But although no other substance will scratch a diamond, a blow from a hammer can fracture it — for, despite its extreme hardness, diamond, like many other gems, is brittle, splitting relatively easily along its crystalline planes. The brittleness of diamonds makes them easy to cleave in the process of gem cutting; it also means that after years of wear in an article of jewelry, a diamond may show tiny cracks and chips near the setting, although its facets will remain unblemished.

In the case of diamond, crystalline structure is paramount in determining hardness. But instead of aggregating in the three-dimensional lattice that is characteristic of diamond, carbon atoms much more commonly stack in flat, six-sided sheets, with the bonds between the layers so weak that they easily slide over one another. The resulting dull mineral, 1.5 on the Mohs scale, is graphite, the inexpensive writing material of pencils.

Although testing for hardness is an easy aid to mineral identification, it has one glaring disadvantage: The owners of costly gems are likely to look with understandable dismay on the idea of having them scratched. Another method, somewhat more sophisticated and considerably more precise, is based on the principle that, in about 250 B.C., according to legend, sent Archimedes leaping from his bath and running in the buff through the streets of Syracuse, in Sicily, shouting *"Eureka!"* — "I have found it!"

At the time, the great Greek mathematician had been confounded in his attempts to ascertain whether a crown belonging to King Hiero II was pure gold or an alloy of gold and silver. In his bath, Archimedes, noting how the water spilled over the tub as he eased himself in, was smitten by an inspiration: that a body immersed in water displaces an amount equal to its volume. He quickly realized that by immersing the crown in water, he could determine its volume: Since he knew that gold and silver have different densities, he could divide the crown's weight by its volume, thus calculating its density, and hence its purity.

The most familiar unit of gemstone measurement is the carat, which equals one fifth of a gram (about the same weight, incidentally, as a seed of the Mediterranean carob tree, from which the word "carat" probably comes). But because the carat is an expression not of size but of weight, a one-carat emerald is notably larger than a one-carat ruby. Behind that apparent discrepancy lies the fact that ruby's density or, in the terminology

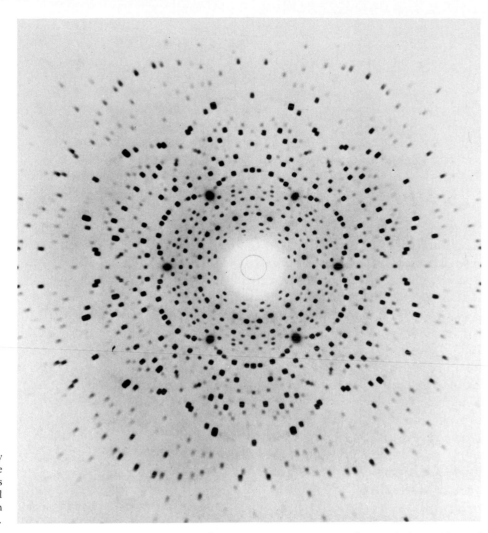

An X-ray diffraction photograph created by training X-rays on a sample of beryl evinces the mineral's crystalline geometry. The rays are deflected by atoms in the gem's hexagonal crystal structure and interact to produce an array of beams that radiates in six directions.

most commonly used, its specific gravity — the ratio of its weight to that of an equal volume of water — is higher than that of emerald. Specific gravity varies widely among gems and is important to gemstone identification.

A convenient method for determining specific gravity is based on a physical law formulated by Archimedes long after his legendary bath: A body immersed in a fluid loses as much in weight as the weight of an equal volume of fluid. With a specially designed balance, a gem is first weighed in air, then suspended in water and weighed again. The stone's specific gravity is found by dividing its weight in air by the loss of weight in water.

But water's surface tension — the cohesive quality of its molecules that makes its surface behave in some respects like a tough membrane — inhibits accurate readings of the weight of a small submerged gemstone. Therefore, another technique, called the heavy liquids method, is often substituted. A number of fluids are far denser than water; methylene iodide, for instance, has a specific gravity of 3.32. A gem that is less dense than a heavy liquid in which it is immersed will float; if the gem is denser than the fluid, it will sink. One way of determining specific gravity is to find a heavy liquid in which the stone will hang suspended, or sink very slowly — an indication of equal density, hence equal specific gravity.

For example, the potential purchaser of a yellow gemstone may be in doubt as to whether it is a relatively inexpensive citrine or a more valuable topaz. But the stone can be readily identified by determining its specific gravity, since standard mineralogical tables show that the two possibilities are significantly different in density: Citrine is 2.65 and topaz ranges from 3.5 to 3.6. If the stone sinks slowly when immersed in methylene iodide, the gemstone is topaz. For good King Hiero, the outcome of Archimedes' discovery was less fortunate: His crown turned out to be an alloy.

Although density can hardly be considered a glamorous quality, it is nevertheless a crucial factor in determining how minerals catch and respond to light. And of that radiant relationship is born the beauty — the fire and dazzle, the luminous glow, the galaxy of superb colors — that has placed gemstones among the most pleasing and precious of human possessions.

When light strikes a solid in which the atoms are aligned so that the energy of the rays passes readily from electron to electron, most of the light is transmitted, and the material is transparent. If, however, the atoms are arranged so as to bar the passage of light, the substance is opaque — although its surface may be highly lustrous and reflective, or it may be dull. Other substances are translucent; that is, they transmit some light, but not enough to allow individual objects to be distinguished through them. Gemstones range across this whole gamut: Gem-quality amethyst, emerald and diamond are transparent; opal is milkily translucent, and lapis lazuli, for all its rich hue, is opaque.

But even transparent substances do not allow light to pass through unaffected. As light rays travel from air into a denser medium, they slow abruptly, sometimes to a fraction of their ordinary velocity. At the same moment, they bend. This change of direction and velocity, known as refraction, is governed partly by the density of the substance, and also by the nature of its crystalline lattice.

Since these qualities vary among minerals, it follows that each mineral refracts light to a specific degree. The amount of bending and slowing imposed on light by a given mineral is expressed as its refractive index, which corresponds to the ratio of the speed of light in air to its speed in the material. Measured by an instrument called a refractometer, refractive indices can serve as an accurate aid to gemstone identification. Diamond has a remarkably high index rating of 2.42 (which means that light travels 2.42 times as fast in air as it does in the gem), while quartz's is a mere 1.54 to 1.55. Among red gemstones that might otherwise be mistaken for one another, the refractive indices are revealing: that of tourmaline ranges from 1.62 to 1.64, spinel from 1.71 to 1.73 and ruby from 1.76 to 1.77.

But there are other surprising aspects to the interplay of light and transparent substances, as Isaac Newton — one of the pioneers of optics — learned in 1666 when he aimed a narrow beam of white light into a prism and found that it split into all the colors of the rainbow. What Newton had observed was the phenomenon now known as dispersion. In every refractive material, the degree to which light is bent varies somewhat with the wavelength of the light. But in highly dispersive materials, the variation is extreme. The constituent colors of white light, varying slightly in wavelength, emerge from such substances on radically different paths. Among the most dispersive of all gemstones is diamond, and to that property it owes its fire — the myriad twinkles of color into which it can split pedestrian white light. Toward the other end of the scale is topaz, which has little dispersion and must depend on other qualities for its appeal. Zircon offers a special case. A compound of the element zirconium with traces of radioactive elements, it occurs in two forms. In its so-called high form, it has much of the flash of diamond. But in its low form, radioactivity has broken down the crystalline structure, causing a lowering of the refractive index and a loss of dispersion; the result is a very plain cousin indeed.

Another quirky optical consequence of crystalline structure is double refraction. Interacting with the planes of atoms within the crystal, light is very often refracted in two directions. The phenomenon is surprisingly common among gems and other minerals: Every system of crystals, except those structured on the simplest possible unit, the cube, exhibits this peculiarity. One dramatic example of double refraction is found in Iceland spar, a water-clear variety of calcite that, when placed on a printed page, reveals twin images of the words beneath it. Among gemstones, emerald, ruby, sapphire and zircon in its high form are notable for double refraction. Zircon and clear sapphire can thus be distinguished from diamond—similarly colorless but singly refractive—because, when viewed from the front, the lesser stones display the edges of the back facets as double images.

Refraction, with its attendant phenomena of dispersion and brilliance, is a product of the basic composition and structure of a crystalline mineral. But other gem properties that are just as notable may result from impurities or imperfections in the basic crystal. Among those properties is color, produced when a mineral absorbs some but not all wavelengths of white light, thus disturbing its color balance and giving prominence to a certain hue.

Sapphire and ruby are both forms of the mineral corundum, which in its pure state is colorless. Only because the corundum is tainted with an occasional atom of chromium does ruby glow bright red, and only because of traces of iron or titanium (or both) does sapphire shine in its splendid array of colors—ranging from shades of yellow, green, pink and purple to, most prized of all, a striking cornflower blue. Oddly, the same element, chromium, that stains a ruby also accounts for the rich green of emerald; the difference in hue is the result of differing crystalline structures, which affect the absorptive qualities of the chromium.

Imperfections in crystalline structure can also create color on their own. Smoky quartz does not differ in composition from clear quartz; its color is the consequence of electrons that have been knocked askew by natural radiation, creating an irregularity in the crystalline lattice that impedes the passage of certain light wavelengths. The smoky tint can be dispelled by heating the quartz until the displaced electrons jump back into place. Similarly, artificially applied radiation will add or improve color in many gems by changing their crystalline structure: With a heavy dose of radiation, a diamond can be suffused with a deep green color rarely found in nature.

Impurities and imperfections can enhance the play of light in a gem as well as its color. Chrysoberyl—a rare and lovely gemstone occurring in shades of green and yellow—as well as beryl, tourmaline and quartz, may show a slit of glowing light that is reminiscent of a cat's eye. Indeed, the name of the phenomenon, chatoyancy, is taken from the French words "chat," for "cat," and "oeil," for "eye." The cat's-eye band is best seen under a focused source of light, for it consists of reflections from thousands of tiny parallel inclusions, or foreign substances, that congregated within the crystal as it formed. Most often, the inclusions are needle-like particles of the mineral rutile; the greater the number of inclusions and the thinner they are, the finer the cat's-eye glow is likely to be.

At other times, however, the tiny needles may align themselves in several directions. In corundum, minuscule bundles of rutile are sometimes arranged in three sets, paralleling the planes of the hexagonal crystalline

Three stones illustrate the differing abilities of gems to transmit light. Topaz *(top)* is transparent and reveals visual details such as the weave of the cloth beneath the gem. Rose quartz *(center)*, which is translucent, allows light to pass through but obscures shapes behind it. Malachite *(bottom)*, an opaque gemstone, bars light completely and owes its luster to surface reflections alone.

structure and intersecting one another at angles of 120 degrees. The reflected result, a phenomenon called asterism, is a sparkling six-rayed star — and some individual star sapphires and rubies are ranked among the world's most renowned gemstones.

Moonstone is another gem that profits by its imperfections. Not a pure mineral at all but a clouded composite of thin, alternating layers of two related minerals, moonstone glows a ghostly blue because of a phenomenon called schiller. Both components are colorless, but the internal layers act much like a film of oil on a wet street, distilling ordinary light into vivid color. The peacock hues of opal result from an even more complex internal structure consisting of tiny spheres of silica — the same drab compound that makes up ordinary sand — cemented together in a dense, regular array. Light reflected and scattered by the fine internal latticework of spheres and intervening spaces emerges, through an optical phenomenon known as diffraction, as a series of brilliant colors that flash as the opal is rotated.

Eerie effects can be produced when the impurities in certain gemstones respond to light wavelengths that are not normally visible. When placed under short-wave ultraviolet light in a dark room, ruby commonly glows red as electrons absorb the invisible energy and reemit it as visible light. The fabled Hope diamond exhibits an extraordinary delayed reaction to short-wave radiation. Exposure to ultraviolet light causes the Hope to glow dimly, as do many other gems. But when the light source is taken away, the agitated atoms of the great diamond release stored energy to produce a brilliant scarlet phosphorescence.

For a spectacular show of dazzling light, few if any gemstones can surpass strontium titanate, a compound whose colorless crystal has four times the dispersive power of diamond. Yet strontium titanate is wanting in most of the properties that bestow value on gemstones. Compared with diamond's queenly beauty, strontium titanate has the flash of a streetwalker. Its hardness on the Mohs scale is only 5 to 6, rendering it incapable of enduring long or hard wear. Worst of all, it is only as rare as its human manufacturers, who market it under such names as Fabulite and Wellington Diamond, wish it to be — for strontium titanate is an imitation gem.

Imitation gems are as old as technology itself: As early as 5000 B.C., the Egyptians fashioned ornaments of faience, a glazed ceramic that could be tinted to resemble turquoise. By 1600 B.C., cut glass had appeared, masquerading as any number of transparent gemstones. During Roman times, in fact, a shortage of the material made glass trinkets more highly prized than many natural gems.

The history of composite gems, another form of gemstone imitation involving the artificial combination of substances, is nearly as long, and these so-called doublets and triplets remain ubiquitous today. Imitation emerald triplets, one of the most common composites, often consist of layers of colorless beryl, joined with a film of cement containing a green dye. Opal doublets — not so brazenly deceptive — are topped with a thin layer of genuine opal, but the base of the gem may be glass or onyx.

By far the greatest quantity of human ingenuity has been spent in efforts to imitate diamond. Imitations crowd the market today, ranging in quality from cut-glass baubles to eight other, more credible laboratory products such as strontium titanate and two sparkly substances with formidable

When white light strikes the facets at the top of a brilliant-cut diamond *(top)*, its component colors are bent, or refracted, at different angles in a phenomenon that is known as dispersion. Thus separated, the hues are reflected internally and emerge through the top of the gem as a shower of color.

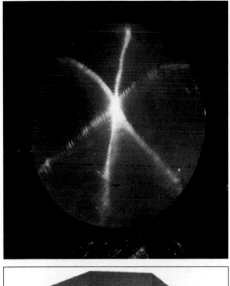

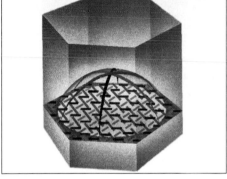

The six-rayed glow, or asterism, of a star ruby *(top)* is produced by the reflections from myriad tiny needles that are oriented along the three horizontal directions of the ruby's internal structure. (In the diagram, the three directions and their corresponding reflections are identified by color.) To center the star on the gem, the gem cutter must center the dome on the vertical axis of the original crystal.

chemical names mercifully shortened to YAG and GGG. But a substance called cubic zirconia takes imitation to a high art. Cubic zirconia can be produced in batches of 100 pounds and sold wholesale for a few dollars a carat, yet its optical properties make it almost impossible to distinguish from diamond by an untrained eye; it has about the same amount of fire, is only slightly less refractive and is durable enough for long wear.

But no imitation gem can hope for total deception — even cubic zirconia can readily be unmasked by its high specific gravity — because imitations differ from the real thing in chemical composition and crystalline structure. A more recent line of endeavor has attempted to duplicate natural gemstones in every detail — to make in the laboratory what nature creates in the depths of the planet.

A laboratory-grown ruby was the first triumph of gem synthesis. In 1837, the French chemist Marc Gaudin melted chemical compounds that decomposed to produce aluminum oxide, or alumina, the basic chemical constituent of ruby, with a touch of chromium added to the mixture for color. He obtained a few flecks of a red material. Milky and prone to cracking, the particles were in fact ruby, but Gaudin believed he had produced nothing more than ruby-colored glass. Encouraged by what seemed a near-miss, French chemists tried throughout the second half of the 19th Century to devise a method of melting and gradual cooling that would yield gem-sized crystals. Finally, in 1902, Auguste Verneuil, a professor at the Museum of Natural History in Paris, announced an unqualified success. Not only is Verneuil's technique still used, it has been adapted to the manufacture of other gemstones as well.

To make ruby, Verneuil's system uses a special furnace fired with hydrogen and oxygen. In carefully controlled amounts, powdered aluminum oxide, with a trace of chromium added, is sieved into a tube fed by oxygen; the mixture is then charged with hydrogen and fed into the combustion chamber. Melting as it falls through the flame, the aluminum oxide drips from the tube's outlet onto a clay pedestal. There, it cools into a single crystal of ruby known as a boule. Only a few hours are required to form a synthetic ruby of several hundred carats — identical in chemical composition and atomic structure to natural ruby. From making rubies by Verneuil's flame-fusion technique, it was a simple step to synthesizing sapphires: Titanium and iron, the usual coloring agents of sapphire, are substituted for the chromium in the mix of aluminum oxide.

More recently, an exotic touch has been added to the Verneuil process. To the basic recipe of aluminum oxide with chromium or titanium and iron, between .1 and .3 per cent of titanium oxide is added. After the boule is formed, it is reheated to more than 2,000° F., causing the titanium oxide particles to array themselves in innumerable needle-like inclusions that reflect light as in a star sapphire or ruby. But there is a major drawback: The stars thus formed are so much clearer and brighter than those occurring in nature that they are a dead giveaway of the gems' synthetic origin.

When magnesium oxide is substituted for part of the aluminum oxide in the feed material for the Verneuil apparatus, the result is colorless synthetic spinel. Various coloring ingredients are usually added to the formula to produce substances that retain the composition and structure of spinel but can be sold as imitation emerald, aquamarine, blue zircon, green tourmaline — or even as milky moonstone.

Imitating Nature's Mineral Artistry

In laboratories and factories, technicians can now create conditions of heat and chemical activity similar to those that give birth to gemstones deep within the earth. The result is synthetic gems, identical to their natural counterparts in chemistry and crystalline structure, and so similar in appearance that a microscope is often needed to tell them apart.

The chemical ingredients for a man-made gem are easy to obtain, since most gems consist of relatively common chemical compounds. The art of gem synthesis lies in the technique by which the gem material is liquefied, in a melt or a solution, and then allowed to crystallize slowly and evenly.

The so-called flame-fusion method, based on melting and gradual cooling, has been used to grow crystals of about 100 minerals and gems, including ruby, sapphire and spinel. But the ingredients of some gems decompose during the fierce heating needed to melt them, and others have extraordinarily high melting points. Such gems — among them emerald — are often manufactured by another process, called flux growth. In this process, the gem is crystallized from a solution of its constituents in a molten bath of a solvent, or flux — such as lead fluoride, boron oxide or lithium oxide.

Because of peculiarities in their internal structure, some gems cannot be synthesized by ordinary crystal growth. Opal, an orderly arrangement of minute, closely packed spheres of silica, is created in the laboratory by precipitating silica spheres through a chemical reaction, allowing them to settle to the bottom of the reaction vessel and then compressing and bonding them to form a compact and sturdy matrix.

Artful as they are, synthetic gems nevertheless bear hallmarks of their laboratory origin: an array of microscopic inclusions and growth marks that, as shown in the photomicrographs opposite, contrast tellingly with the blemishes and inclusions of natural gems.

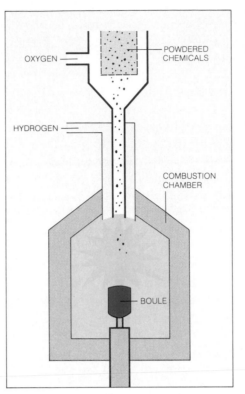

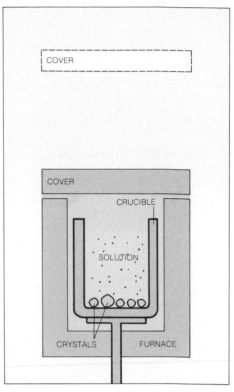

FLAME-FUSION GROWTH OF RUBY
The chemical ingredients of ruby — aluminum oxide with a chromium coloring agent — sift from a hopper at the top of the apparatus shown above into a jet of oxygen. In a combustion chamber, the oxygen combines with hydrogen in a 4,000° F. flame — hot enough to melt the powdered ingredients, which shower onto a ceramic rod at the base of the furnace. There the material solidifies and accumulates in a rounded crystalline mass known as a boule, such as the half-inch ruby boule below.

FLUX GROWTH OF EMERALD
A saturated solution of emerald's chemical ingredients is produced by combining compounds of beryllium, aluminum and silicon with a flux, or solvent, and heating the mixture to 1,500° F. in an electric furnace (*above*). As the mixture cools, gem crystals begin to precipitate out at the bottom of the platinum crucible containing the solution, eventually forming clusters of emeralds (*below*).

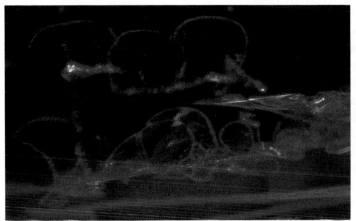

NATURAL RUBY (60×)
In the interior of a natural ruby, wing-shaped fractures mark the boundaries between separate, interlayered crystals, which are joined at common crystal planes to form a single gemstone.

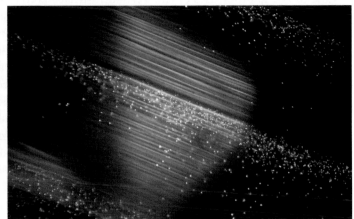

SYNTHETIC RUBY (45×)
The laboratory origin of this ruby is evidenced by bands of differing color — the result of varying amounts of pigment in the molten gem material as it accreted — and by galaxies of trapped gas bubbles.

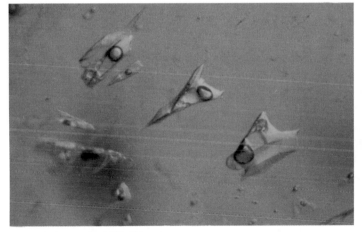

NATURAL EMERALD (100×)
The interior of a natural emerald is pocked with cavities containing liquid, gas bubbles and particles of solid — indications of the chaotic geologic environment in which the emerald took shape.

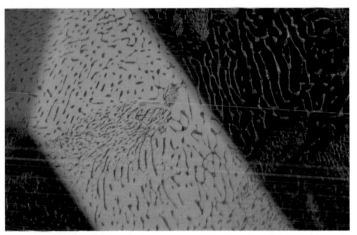

SYNTHETIC EMERALD (40×)
A "flux fingerprint," typical of flux-grown emeralds, marks the site of a crack that opened during crystal formation, then filled with new emerald deposits that trapped threadlike veins of unmelted flux.

NATURAL OPAL (20×)
A natural opal displays a pattern of irregular, interlocking grains, a reflection of the granular structure of the mineral in whose interstices the developing opal took shape.

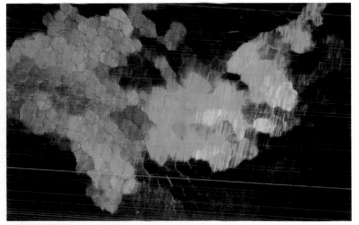

SYNTHETIC OPAL (40×)
The characteristic honeycomb structure of a synthetic opal is formed when its component silica particles settle out of solution, giving rise to a jelly-like mass that shrinks and crazes like drying mud.

MOONSTONE
ZIRCON
AMETHYST

SAPPHIRE
RUBY

OPAL

PERIDOT

ALLUVIUM

TURQUOISE

LIMESTONE

SHALE

SANDSTONE

SPODUMENE
(KUNZITE)

BERYL

AQUAMARINE

TOURMALINE

EMERALD

MARBLE

SCHIST

GNEISS

TOPAZ

GRANITE

MAGMA

PRECIOUS PRODUCTS OF THE ROCK CYCLE

TANZANITE

JADEITE

GARNET

CHRYSOBERYL

In the great life cycle of the earth, molten rock rises from the depths of the planet, cools and solidifies, and endures eons of reworking by the shifting crust and surface weather, only to make its way at last back into the interior to melt once more. Gemstones can be regarded as incidental by-products of this monumental geologic recycling process.

Conditions favorable for gemstones occur when rising magma first solidifies, at about 2,000° F., into igneous rock, such as granite. If the magma cools very slowly, in cavities and interstices far below the surface (*far left*), large mineral crystals are likely to form in it. Magma that reaches the surface quickly in a volcanic eruption cools too fast to permit crystallization, though this extruded rock may contain gems that were formed in the depths.

The processes of erosion slowly but irresistibly break down igneous rock on the surface, wash it away and redeposit it in the form of sediments or alluvium (*left center*). Often seasoned by organic matter, sediments are in time compressed again into rock. Although a few species of gemstones are formed in sediments under special conditions, these stratified deposits are mostly repositories for crystals that have been released from igneous rock by erosion.

However, layers of sedimentary rock thousands of feet thick may be further compressed and heated when the earth's crust is folded into mountains (*left*), or when molten magma intrudes from below. In these circumstances the rock is reforged into an entirely new material called metamorphic rock; schist, gneiss and marble are common examples. And in the process of metamorphism, still other species of gems are created.

In time, all this rock may be eroded and washed with other sediments into the sea, accumulating on one of the great oceanic plates. These massive, continuously moving pieces of the earth's crust, called tectonic plates, eventually push their way beneath adjacent plates, returning the thoroughly blended rock — and undoubtedly many fabulous undiscovered gems — to the infernal depths.

The slow, never-ending processes that move the earth's crust back into the depths for recycling are indicated by the arrows in this illustration.

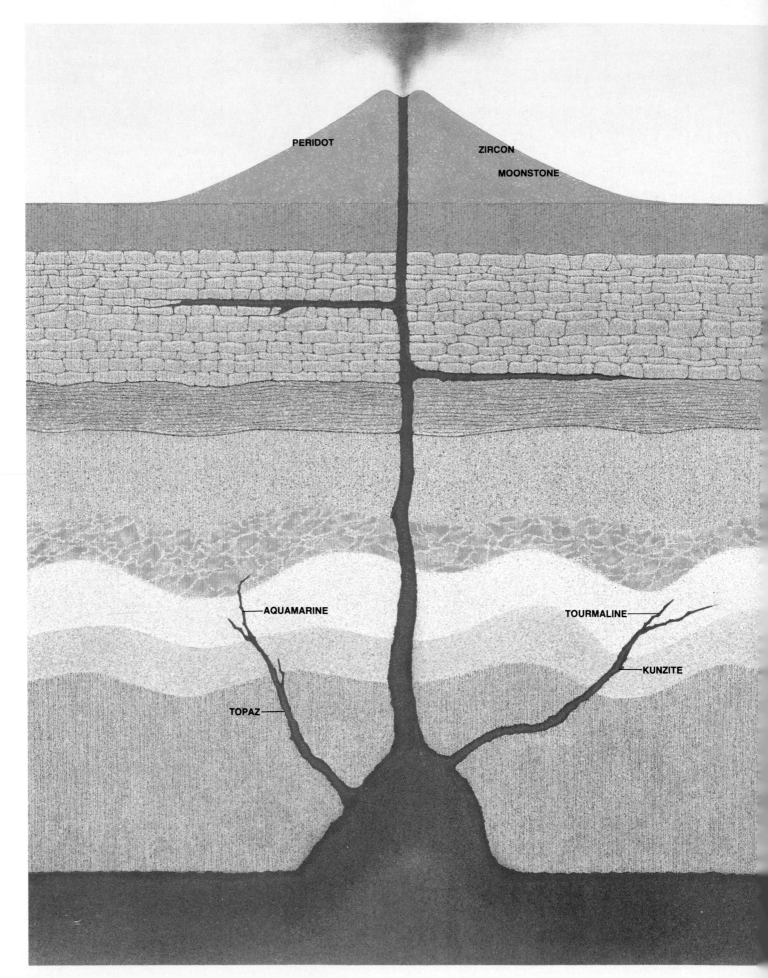

PERIDOT

ZIRCON

MOONSTONE

AQUAMARINE

TOURMALINE

KUNZITE

TOPAZ

The Alchemy of Liquid Stone

The earth's crust is a thin veneer on an ocean of searing magma, and the majority of precious gems have precipitated out of this primeval brew. Not all magma is the same, however: The texture, chemistry and density of the parent magma determines the type of gemstones that form.

Gabbro, a magma that has little silicon but is rich in iron and magnesium, gives rise to the formation of some peridot, zircons and sapphires; and diamonds are found in a chemically related magma that in its solid form is called kimberlite. These magmas are dense and generally flow underneath a lighter type of magma, which is found directly below the continents.

The more buoyant molten mixture above the gabbro is a silica-rich granitic magma — molten granite. Enriched by ingredients that are drawn from the solid rock just above it, granitic magma becomes the most prolific producer of gems when it forces its way into fissures in the solid crust where it solidifies into gem-bearing formations known as pegmatites. Natural jewel boxes, pegmatites provide the space and the chemical isolation necessary for the formation of pure mineral crystals.

Although most gems are relatively small, one crystal of white, industrial-grade spodumene that was found in a pegmatite in South Dakota was 40 feet long and five feet wide and weighed more than eight tons.

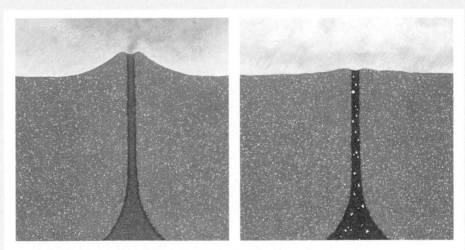

Formed under tremendous pressure deep in the mantle, diamond crystals are held together by the strongest known atomic bonding. Their strength preserves them as violent upwellings of magma create vertical columns of igneous rock, called kimberlite pipes. The pipes and their precious cargo are slowly uncovered by erosion.

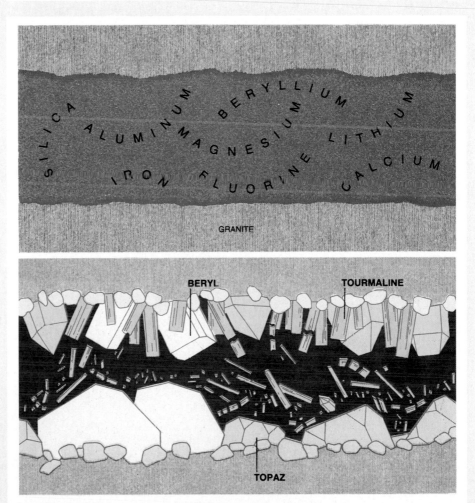

SILICA ALUMINUM BERYLLIUM MAGNESIUM IRON FLUORINE LITHIUM CALCIUM

GRANITE

BERYL TOURMALINE

TOPAZ

Incapable of stabilizing within the predominant crystal structures in granite, rare elements separate from the granitic magma and form rocks called pegmatites. Mixing with gases and water (center), the exotic minerals form large, pure crystals in the space created by the volatile gases (above). Rich treasure troves, pegmatites may yield many gemstones, including topaz, tourmaline and beryl.

Magic Transformations in Metamorphic Rock

When the solid rock in the earth's crust is brought almost to its melting point, it becomes unstable and many of its minerals recrystallize without melting. The result is a new, metamorphic type of rock and a variety of new gemstones.

Metamorphism occurs in two ways: by contact, when a tongue of molten rock intrudes into solid rock layers; or throughout a large region when portions of the crust are folded and distorted by the movement of tectonic plates, the compression producing the requisite heat and pressure.

Metamorphism turns sandstone into a granular rock called quartzite, and shale into a fine-grained slate called hornfels. And in some cases impurities in the rock recrystallize to form new gems. For example, as metamorphism cooks limestone, changing it into marble, aluminum in the limestone may recrystallize with silica to form rubies or sapphires.

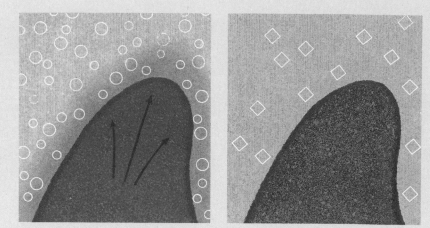

Penetrating a layer of cooler sedimentary rock, intrusive granitic magma increases the temperature of the solid rock to more than 1,800° F. *(above, left)*. Excited by the heat energy, the atoms in the sedimentary minerals break free of the crystal structure and reform *(above, right)* into a new, more stable structure.

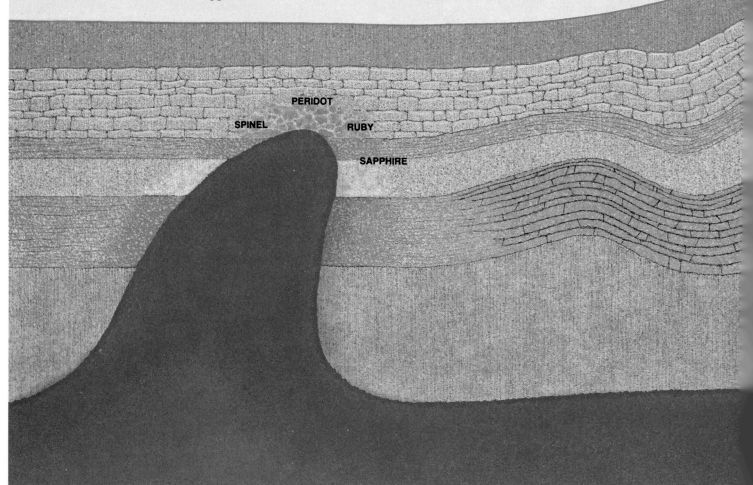

PERIDOT

SPINEL

RUBY

SAPPHIRE

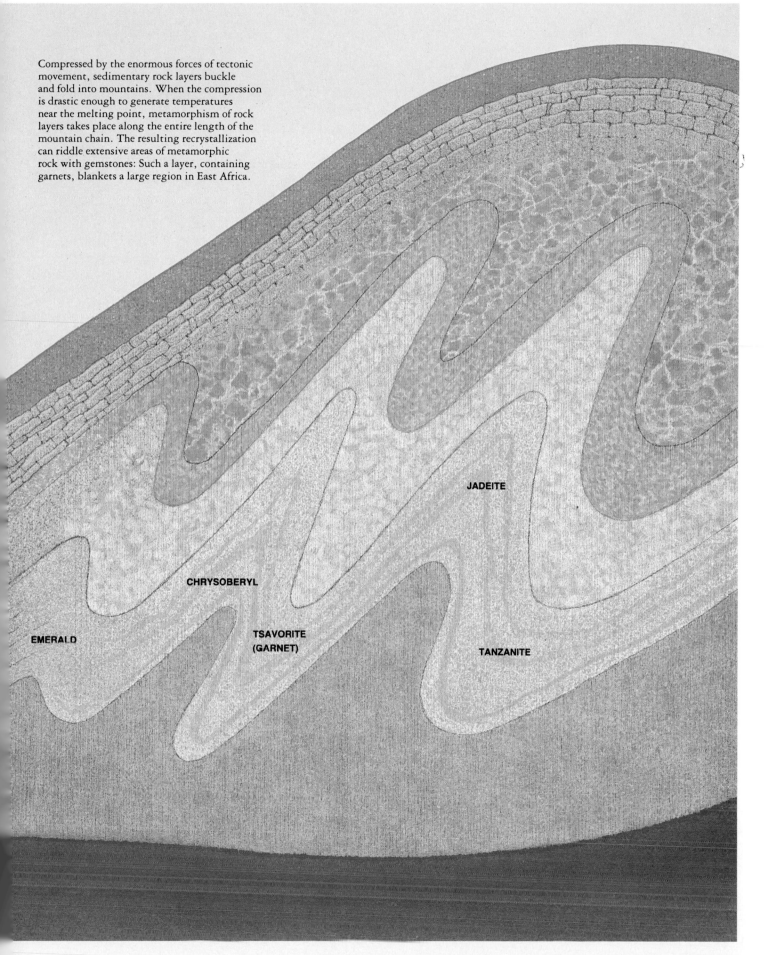

Compressed by the enormous forces of tectonic movement, sedimentary rock layers buckle and fold into mountains. When the compression is drastic enough to generate temperatures near the melting point, metamorphism of rock layers takes place along the entire length of the mountain chain. The resulting recrystallization can riddle extensive areas of metamorphic rock with gemstones: Such a layer, containing garnets, blankets a large region in East Africa.

JADEITE

CHRYSOBERYL

EMERALD

TSAVORITE
(GARNET)

TANZANITE

Buried Treasure in the Sediments

Most rocks disintegrate when they are exposed to the action of wind and, especially, water. When the rock material erodes, the hardier gem crystals are uncovered: Being much denser, most gems resist weathering far better than their rock surroundings.

Once exposed by erosion, gemstones are washed away in the gravel remains of their host rock. This gem-rich detritus eventually accumulates in what are called alluvial, or placer, deposits — the major sources of the world's gems — in distant riverbeds, lakes or oceans. Indeed, the island of Sri Lanka in the Indian Ocean is essentially one large alluvial deposit left behind by the erosion of ancient metamorphic rock. Because of its dazzling yield of sapphires and many other gems, Sri Lanka is often called the Gem Island.

Only a few precious gems are actually formed during the processes of weathering and sedimentation. Turquoise, for instance, forms when aluminum and phosphorus are leached out of igneous rock and mix with traces of copper, which imparts a characteristic green-blue coloring. As the deposits of these elements build up in a solution of water, the minerals slowly crystallize.

Opal forms in arid, alkaline environments when rain water leaches silica out of igneous surface rocks; then the solution finds its way into open spaces in the underlying rock. Gaps are often left when organic matter, such as wood, bone or shell, decomposes. The silica replaces the organic matter, but it does not crystallize. Instead, microscopic spheres of silica form into regular masses, somewhat like tightly packed marbles.

OPAL

ZIRCON

MOONSTONE

PERIDOT

Rock thrust up by tectonic forces is sculpted by weathering processes into jagged peaks (*far right*) as gem-bearing sediments are eventually washed into the valley (*center*). There, erosion continues to break down and transport the rock, forming the gem-rich alluvial deposits that are found in the beds of streams and rivers and in bedrock cavities beneath deserts (*right*).

Most sediment deposits show a marked succession of materials that is often visible in a steep riverbank. The heavier detritus is seen at the lowest levels, the fine light debris on the surface. Because they are dense and immune to most erosion processes, gems tend to work their way down to the coarse lower layers.

SAPPHIRE

RUBY

TURQUOISE

Chapter 3

THE LURE OF COLORED STONES

An ancient Burmese legend tells of a giant eagle, soaring high over the Mogok valley in quest of food. Far below, the eagle spied what appeared to be raw meat "the color of the brightest, purest blood." Swooping down to earth, the great bird tore at the object with its talons, but the rock-hard surface resisted its most avid efforts. Not until the eagle approached the target slowly and reverently, recognizing that it was a sacred red stone created "from the fire and blood of the earth," was the bird able to pluck the stone up and return to its aerie.

The narrow, 20-mile-long Mogok valley, hidden in the fetid jungle about 70 miles northeast of Mandalay, is a place where such legends seem credible. Its past lost in antiquity, its present shrouded by an oppressive secrecy, its symbol an inscrutable Buddha ensconced on a hilltop and adorned with precious gemstones, Mogok is renowned as the home of the world's finest rubies — stones so intensely red that their color, and only theirs, merits the descriptive term of "pigeon blood." Mogok's mines were already ancient when the 13th Century Mongol khans scourged Burma; 15th Century criminals were sentenced by the King of the Golden Land, as Burma was called, to labor in the mines, and their bones became part of Mogok's rotting earth.

Mogok resists change. After annexing Upper Burma in 1886, the British attempted to apply the latest technology to the gleaning of rubies from Mogok's gravels. A corporation was set up and heavy machinery was transported at immense cost along a road constructed through jungle infested with wild beasts, including tigers of large appetite, and human predators. After 40 years of desperate effort, the British company went broke — a common fate for anyone trying to use modern methods in the primeval places where colored gemstones are almost always found. Mogok's native miners soon reverted to their old ways, which consisted mainly of digging holes in the ground by hand.

Mogok's natural inaccessibility was enhanced with bureaucratic barriers after the 1962 seizure of power by Burma's xenophobic socialist dictator, General Ne Win. The general not only nationalized the mines, claiming all they produced as property of the state, but forbade foreigners to visit Mogok and required native Burmese to apply for special permission from the government to be in the area. He made the unauthorized possession of so much as a shovel in Mogok's environs a crime and installed a division of Army troops to enforce his edicts. But while there are 13 government mines, there are a hundred private operations scattered throughout Burma.

Amethyst crystals glint from the muck moments after the stone overlying the gemstones was shattered and removed. The pit is located in the gem-rich state of Rio Grande do Sul, Brazil.

"Soldiers are human beings too," says a former Mogok valley resident; for enough money "they will look the other way."

Not the least of Mogok's mysteries is what Ne Win then decided to do with its rubies. They all but vanished from government-sponsored auctions, thereby inspiring frequent rumors that the Mogok mines had at last played out. But that notion continued to be contradicted sporadically by the appearance of fine pigeon bloods brought out of Burma by smugglers from government and private mines alike. "The Burmese government," says a Bangkok gem dealer, "pays the miners only $10 a day, so when they hit a big stone, they swallow it and afterward bring it to the border, even if they have to walk for a month." Adds a trader in Mandalay: "Most everybody in Mogok is out there digging by himself. They'll have a grinding wheel in the jungle and stealthily cut and polish the stones right there — no one would dare have a grinding wheel in town — and then they smuggle them out."

Taking well-worn jungle trails, beset by guerrillas who exact "customs tax" payments, the few smugglers who make it out eventually arrive in Thailand, where they are met at the border by international traders who view the illicit traffic as an inconvenient but necessary part of their commercial life. But Thailand is much more than a mere terminus for contraband. In what has become a traditional pattern, when one major source is for some reason diminished or cut off, another moves in to slake the insatiable human thirst for colored gemstones. Thai rubies, once known rather contemptuously as "Siams," are darker than Mogok's, frequently tinged with brown or violet and, because they contain traces of iron, considerably less fluorescent. But they are available — and Thailand today provides an estimated 70 per cent of the world's gem-quality rubies.

The treasure comes from mine sites like the one near the village of Bo Rai in Thailand's Trat province, where the worked earth appears as a raw red scar against the hillside jungle. Under the watchful eyes of armed mine owners, laborers play a high-pressure hose against the slope, washing off mud and gravel, which are then piped into a sluice box where other workers search through the debris.

In Bo Rai itself, ramshackle wooden buildings line the streets, men with pistols jammed into their belts dicker loudly for gems, and howling motorbikes serve as status symbols for those who have struck it rich. Every morning thousands of rubies — most of them too small or too flawed to bring a high price — are displayed at an open-air gem market on tables that are guarded by as many as 20 policemen who may carry American-made M-16 automatic rifles. For the area's population of about 10,000, Bo Rai's police force numbers 140 members. Yet despite this forbidding presence, violence is pervasive; in 1981, for example, there were 50 murders, most of them the result of disputes over mining or land claims.

Life is somewhat more civilized in Chanthaburi, a town of about 20,000 that lies between Bo Rai and the area's other mining districts. Gem merchants, most of them Chinese, have indoor, street-level shops with windows placed to admit the maximum of natural light and with overhead fluorescent tubes to augment it. On the floors above, stones are cut and polished by workers in little factories, using techniques handed down by their ancestors. Parking lots are filled with Mercedes-Benzes used by gem traders from faraway parts of the earth, and restaurant customers haggle over little white

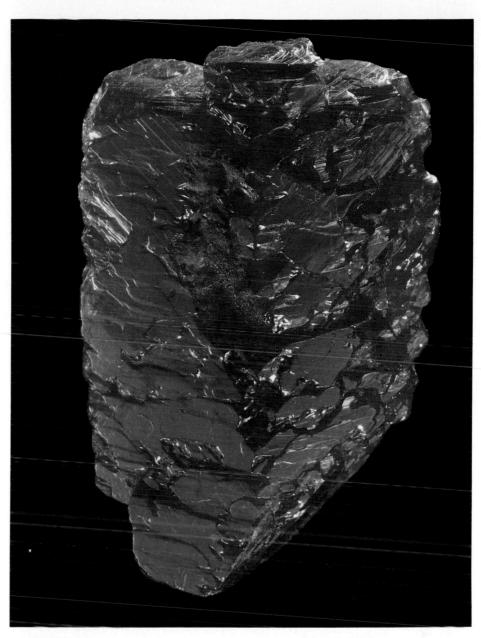

Even in its natural, unpolished state, a 198-carat ruby crystal from the fabled mines of Mogok, Burma, is suffused with an incandescent red. The color, which is peculiar to Mogok rubies, is known as pigeon blood.

packets containing rubies. Yet even in this relatively civilized atmosphere, there are reminders of danger. On the inside of a Chanthaburi hotel-room door a sign edged in red warns: DO NOT OPEN THIS DOOR UNLESS YOU KNOW WHO IS ON THE OTHER SIDE.

With its forbidden mines, jungle tracks and streetside vending tables, its greed and passion and pure love of beautiful things, its dangers and its dreams, the patch of the planet from Mogok to Bo Rai represents in microcosm the whole turbulent world of colored gemstones.

Colored gemstones are to diamonds what fire is to ice. The differences between the two categories of gems are striking at nearly all stages of the progression by which rough stones become finished jewels. Even in its chemical composition, the single-element diamond is of course a paragon of purity, especially when contrasted with the bewildering list of elements found in such gemstones as the multicolored tourmaline. The lengthy chemical formula for tourmaline includes symbols that refer not to elements but to groups of variable components, and it is really only an estimate of the mineral's contents. As the English writer John Ruskin once said, "The chemistry is more like a medieval doctor's prescription than the making of a respectable mineral." Highly developed mechanized methods dominate the production of diamonds, while most of the world's colored gemstones are still harvested by techniques that were old when Cleopatra was bedecking herself with emeralds.

The cutting of a diamond is a science that requires extensive knowledge of the laws of optics and crystallography, and may involve days or even weeks of study of the crystalline structure before the critical cuts are made. But the shaping of colored stones is more an art in which the lapidary's main mission is to show color to best advantage. Cutting may take only a few hours. Symmetry is of so little importance that it is a matter of no great grief if a stone turns out lopsided; small flaws are ignored, or at least accepted. As often as not, the job is done by native artisans who set up shop near the source of the stones — though such gems are frequently recut when they reach Western markets.

Nowhere are the differences more dramatically apparent than in the methods of distribution. Where a monolithic cartel with all the reserve of an international bank distributes diamonds in carefully calculated amounts, the raucous world of colored gemstones is peopled by adventurers, gamblers and individualistic traders such as those who meet the smugglers from Mogok in the jungles of Thailand. Even when governments such as Ne Win's in Burma have attempted to impose upon the production and trade of colored gemstones the same sort of order that has for so long characterized commerce in diamonds, their efforts for the most part have increased the confusion. To be sure, scarcities created both by design and by bureaucratic bungling have raised prices to a point where the best rubies and emeralds presently bring more than their diamond equivalents. But the pricing of colored gems, as an American jeweler concedes, has been "somewhat disorganized. There are no pricing guidelines."

Even the search for deposits of colored gemstones is an endeavor of boundless frustration that must be pursued in hostile environments with scant help from scientific principles. Yet for all the hazards and hardships that attend them, the fiery bits of mineral exert an irresistible attraction.

Late one afternoon in 1981, laborers on a construction gang building a road in central Sri Lanka dropped their tools and gathered around a fellow worker who had just picked up a pebble. When it was discovered to be a sapphire, government officials immediately ordered all work on the road stopped; miners were brought in, and they have ever since been mining gemstones from a widening pit — while motorists detour around the area on an old dirt path.

Sri Lanka, formerly named Ceylon, is a small island of 25,000 square miles in the Indian Ocean southeast of the subcontinent. Over many millions of years the country's ancient rock formations have been broken up by erosion, washed seaward by monsoon deluges and deposited as gem-bearing gravel — called *illam* — in the lowlands, especially in the areas around Elahera and Ratnapura, which translates as "city of gems." The gravel deposits are a cornucopia of at least a dozen important species of colored gemstones (diamonds are notably absent from the Sri Lankan trove), including ruby, sapphire, zircon, moonstone, topaz, tourmaline, spinel, garnet and the fascinating variety of chrysoberyl called alexandrite, which is green when viewed in sunlight but turns raspberry red when exposed to artificial light.

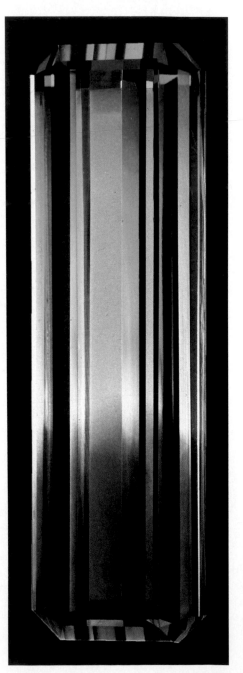

A 42.5-carat tourmaline exhibits a wide range of colors, the result of small variations in chemical composition. Varied colors are found in other gems, but tourmaline is exceptional because it often displays several colors in a single crystal, as in this so-called parti-colored gem.

Of its many treasures, Sri Lanka is most bountifully endowed with sapphires of phenomenal size; to cite just one example, the 362-carat Star of Lanka was found there. Their color runs from the usual hues of yellow and green to rarer tints of tangerine. (The most prized sapphires of all are the lovely cornflower blue gems found only in Kashmir.)

It is an intriguing fact that no one has ever traced Sri Lanka's gemstones back to the rock formations of their birth. Instead, without exception, the gemstones are found in the alluvial gravel of the lowlands. There, in the beds of streams where crocodiles lurk, along the courses of ancient rivers long vanished, in dark jungles where elephants appear as great gray shadows, in snake-infested swamps and even on urban residential properties, the colored gemstones await harvesting.

But the harvesters must pay a price. Following an increasingly prevalent practice, the Sri Lankan government in 1972 assumed control over all gemstone mining operations — to the extent that a homeowner could not legally dig a hole in his own backyard without first purchasing a license from the State Gem Corporation. The strict controls drastically reduced smuggling, consequently increasing the supply of Sri Lankan sapphires in the legitimate commercial markets.

At about the same time, the world sapphire market experienced an influx of gems from two new sources — the bleak Outback of Australia's Queensland, and Yogo Gulch, on the eastern slope of Montana's Little Belt Mountains. Although poles apart both geographically and geologically, the regions share a plentiful supply of gem-quality sapphires and a wildly varied record of success in the marketplace during the century since the gems were discovered.

In the country around the Queensland town of Anakie, ancient alluvial deposits lie atop layers of granite and slate. Although the region is arid, every so often heavy downpours wash away the scanty covering of topsoil and lay bare the gravels in which sapphires nest. When the fields were found, prospectors received less than two cents per carat for their

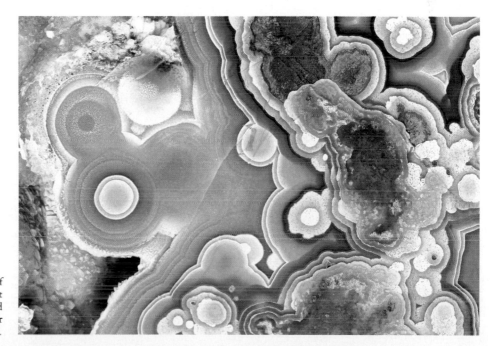

Mexican agate displays the kaleidoscope of colors for which the ornamental stone is best known. The swirling patterns are created by successive deposits of silica carried by water into underground cavities in the bedrock.

From a canopied vantage point, a supervisor surveys miners in the ruby and sapphire fields at Pailin, Kampuchea. The labor involved in processing the gem-rich alluvial gravel is intensive: Only the shaking table, where the gravel is washed and sorted *(center)*, and the pumps that supply it with water are motorized.

The 423-carat Logan sapphire — thought to be the largest blue sapphire in the world — was plucked from the gem gravel of Sri Lanka. The cut of the gem, with its broad top, or table, is designed to display the color of the sapphire rather than to enhance its brilliance.

best blues. Prices rose to more than 20 cents a carat when Australian sapphires came into vogue with the nobility of tsarist Russia, but that popularity lasted only as long as the tsars did. Worldwide demand surged with the prosperity of the 1960s, and the price of Australian sapphires skyrocketed to $100 a carat.

The products of Yogo Gulch in central Montana are the world's only major gem-quality sapphires that are not found loose in gravel but must be extracted from their original matrix, an unusual igneous rock called lamprophyre. Like most gemstones, the Yogo Gulch sapphires were discovered by accident. While seeking gold one day in the late 1800s, a prospector named Jake Hoover took shelter from a hailstorm beneath a ledge of rock. While waiting, he scraped up some gravel that had weathered from the rock and later panned it in nearby Yogo Creek. Finding that it contained gold, Hoover filed a claim.

During the six months that he worked the site, Jake Hoover took out only $700 in gold — and he found small consolation in some pretty little blue pebbles that had evidently become dislodged from the wall of the gulch. Putting them in a pill bottle with some gold, he sent them to a former girl friend who was a schoolteacher in Maine. Much to his surprise, Hoover received a note thanking him for the "sapphires." Jake's response: "What the hell is a sapphire?"

He soon found out. After a Helena lapidary assured him that the stones were "Oriental" sapphires, Hoover filled a cigar box and sent it to Tiffany's in New York. He was promptly rewarded with a check for $3,750 and a request for more stones.

During much of the next century, bad luck (in 1923 a cloudburst washed out the surface facilities), the poor markets of the Depression era and the high cost of quarrying the gemstones forced frequent shutdowns and changes of proprietorship. Since 1980, however, the Yogo Gulch mines have been profitably producing stones that are marketed as "Royal American Sapphires" rather than under their former, somewhat derisive name, "Montanas."

In their deep blue color, the Yogo Gulch sapphires are the equal of any; they are, however, generally small, and they are rarely cut into gems of more than one carat. As for the Australian stones, their size is all that anyone could wish, but the inky darkness of their color holds their price to about 5 per cent of the $2,000 per carat commanded by Sri Lankan sapphires. Such is the enduring association of colored gemstones with the Far East that the Yogo Gulch products are sent to Thailand for cutting, while many Queensland stones go to market in Bangkok to be sold as Orientals.

Emeralds, with a Mohs scale rating of 7.5, are the softest of the four most precious gemstones, and they cannot long withstand the rigors of alluvial processes. Gem-quality emeralds almost always are found in a riverbed before they have traveled far from the host rock formation — or are extracted from the parent rock itself. Since the parent rock is almost always located in the heights of some ancient mountain range, emerald mines are typically wilderness operations, as for instance at the Muzo and Chivor emerald mines in Colombia's Cordillera Oriental, an extension of the Andes. A mere 50 miles apart, the mines offer dramatic testimony to both the physical difficulties and geological subtleties of the quest for colored gems.

Muzo's emeralds occur in white calcite veins that lace thick beds of black shale, while Chivor's are found in feldspar-rich veins through thin deposits of yellowish gray shale or limestone. For reasons that scientists have not yet fathomed, the environment in which the Muzo stones were created was apparently more conducive to inclusions, and the Muzo products are often heavily flawed. In contrast, Chivor's crystals possess a clarity seldom seen in emeralds, and experienced eyes can tell at a glance in which mine a gem was found.

Paradoxically, the Muzo emeralds are considered the more valuable. In chromatic gemstones, color is paramount. And, presumably because of infinitesimal variations in the amounts of the chromic oxide traces that give emeralds their color, Muzo's stones are a magnificent deep, rich bluish green, while those from Chivor are paler, as if they had been diluted by water. Both are exceedingly rare. At Chivor, for example, it has been estimated that the proportion of emeralds to the material that surrounds them is 1 in 90 million — and that less than 1 per cent of the gemstones actually mined are of the best quality.

The conditions under which the stones are extracted are quite different at Chivor and Muzo. Situated higher in the mountains, Chivor is breezy and cool; surrounded closely by high, jungle-clad peaks, Muzo, on the other hand, is miserably hot and stiflingly humid.

At Muzo and Chivor alike, death is a familiar companion; Muzo's present violence is notorious *(pages 100-109),* and Chivor's past is one of unspeakable cruelties. In 1531, when the Spanish conquistador Francisco Pizarro landed on the coast of Peru, he found great stores of superb emeralds there and, later, in Chile and Ecuador. Generous applications of torture, at which the Spaniards were adept, did nothing to lead Pizarro to the source of the green stones because the Indians had acquired them through generations of intertribal trading and had no idea where they had originated.

Not until 1537 did the conquistadors finally trace the emeralds to Chivor, where they ruthlessly set about making up for lost time. More than 1,200 Indians were kept caged within Chivor's mining tunnels, where they were sustained by rations sufficient only to keep them alive and working. Eventually, not even Spain's rulers could continue to tolerate the situation, and they ordered an end to the enslavement of the Indians. The mines were finally abandoned because of severe drops in production, and the jungle closed in; Chivor vanished from the sight and ken of man for more than two centuries. It was rediscovered in 1896 by a Colombian mining engineer using a description of the location he found in a 300-year-old manuscript.

Today, Chivor is open and operating as Colombia's only privately owned emerald mine; Muzo, after being shut down in the 1970s because of the astronomical number of murders and other crimes, is working again, this time on lease from the government. Violence, wholesale pillage and frightful working conditions continue to afflict mining operations, but the use of dynamite and heavy machinery in place of laborers with hand tools contributed to a twentyfold increase in Colombian emerald exports between 1973 and 1978.

Despite its increased production, modern Muzo is a monument to the waste caused by harsh mining methods. (Blasting uncovered the famous 632-carat Patricia emerald at the Chivor mines, but the same charge destroyed a crystal that appeared to have been even larger.) The government

The face of the two-inch-long, 217.8-carat Mogul emerald is embellished with an Islamic prayer in Arabic script. Mined in Colombia, the emerald was engraved in the late 17th Century by the Mogul rulers of India, who may have used it as the centerpiece of a turban pin.

leases the mines for only five years at a time, and the operators tear into the mountain as fast as they can. Dynamite explosions violate the jungle stillness, jackhammers chatter, and bulldozers scuttle in like giant beetles to sweep aside the rubble and expose the veins in which the precious stones are embedded. Of the emeralds that escape ruin by blasting, many are dislodged from the host rock and are overlooked in the mountains of mineral debris that is later shoved over the cliff to be scavenged by the horde of *guaqueros,* or "treasure hunters," waiting far below in the bed of the Río Itoco. In addition to other deficiencies, Muzo's mining work is itself lethally dangerous. "Mud is everywhere," says a gemstone trader, and both men and machines "are constantly slipping and threatening to fall over the side of the cliff."

Chivor's methods are somewhat less hasty. There the hillside is cut in terraced steps, where miners work side by side with sturdy hoes to remove loose dirt, and crowbars, pointed at one end and wedge-shaped at the other, to prize out chunks of the weathered parent rock. When an emerald is found, it is cautiously removed with a sheath knife and, presumably, turned over to an inspector who carries each day's collection in a leather bag. But in these primitive and chaotic conditions, security is haphazard at best and 30 per cent of the mine's production is stolen. The thievery is endlessly inventive; workers may swallow the emeralds or feed them to chickens, which later pay with their necks for having served as temporary repositories. Other stones doubtless fall victim to the blasting sometimes necessary to break up an unusually hard layer of shale or limestone.

However difficult and inefficient the mining methods, the quality of Colombian stones is unequaled by those from any other source. Emeralds from Zimbabwe (formerly Rhodesia), although vivid, are generally small and are nearly always tinged with yellow; even the best crystals from Zambia have a somewhat metallic appearance; and Brazil's are relatively dull.

Brazil is well compensated for this deficiency, however, with a profusion of colored gemstones such as is found nowhere else in the world except in Sri Lanka. The ancient rock formations of 72,000 square miles of northeastern Brazil constitute the earth's largest expanse of pegmatites — subterranean intrusions of magma in which myriad minerals have crystallized. The area has been the scene of pronounced uplifting and folding, which have brought the minerals to the surface; and its annual torrential rains break down and redistribute the gem-laden rock with uncommon vigor.

The resulting deposits of gem gravels are so extensive and contain such stunning varieties of gems that the Brazilian state of Minas Gerais, meaning "General Mines," was named for their bounty. Here are found not only substantial amounts of diamonds and emeralds but abundant aquamarines in uncounted shades of blue (including one found in 1910 that weighed 550,000 carats), many-shaded tourmalines and topaz — both steel blue and the world's only remaining amber-hued imperial topaz. Equal treasures may yet be found in neighboring states that have not been explored so extensively as has Minas Gerais.

In mining the galaxy of colored gemstones found in alluvial deposits, wherever in the world they are found, patience pays off — and the old ways are usually the best. In Burma, for example, men still find jadeite by wading in creeks and detecting the valuable boulders by feel with their bare feet. In many places, mining consists of nothing more than scooping out

Many of the rare and beautiful substances that have long been valued as gems are created by living things, rather than inanimate geological processes.

Amber, for example, is a form of resin that was secreted 30 to 40 million years ago by trees and then transformed by eons of burial into a tough solid. Much of the world's amber is found on beaches along the Baltic Sea — a region once forested with resin-bearing trees.

Some of the other organic gems — pearls, ivory and coral — are harvested more directly from living things. Ivory is the stuff of tusks from such animals as the walrus, the elephant and the hippopotamus. Precious coral consists of the accumulated stony skeletons of tiny marine animals. And pearls, created when certain mollusks deposit concentric layers of secretion around foreign substances lodged in their soft tissues, can be grown, or cultured. A round bead of shell — surgically inserted into the body of the living mollusk — triggers the organism's protective reaction and can be removed a few years later, luminously encased in pearl.

A termite, trapped millions of years ago in pine resin, was embalmed when the resin hardened into amber. The rainbow colors indicate areas of strain created during the insect's death struggle.

A string of beads shows the translucency and mellow hue for which amber has long been treasured: Amber beads have been found in 4,000-year-old graves near Stonehenge, England.

Off the coast of Japan, an *ama* — a female pearl diver — keeps a wary eye on the scything fin of a passing shark while depositing a pearl oyster in a floating basket. The oysters she collects from the sea bottom at depths of up to 25 feet will be used to produce cultured pearls.

Identical in appearance to their natural counterparts, cultured pearls display the silvery sheen, or orient, that is characteristic of the gem. When light strikes the tiny, overlapping plates of the pearl's crystalline material it scatters and creates the optical effect.

Precious coral branches nestle in the collecting basket of *Star II,* a small submarine used for gathering coral in the waters off Hawaii. Unlike the reef-building corals of shallow seas, which have little value as a gem material, precious corals are found at depths of up to 1,600 feet.

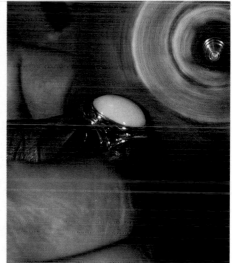

A coral ring gets a final buffing after being fashioned in the rounded, or cabochon, style commonly used for coral jewelry. The colors of precious coral range from white through shades of pink to oxblood and black.

An Alaskan walrus displays ivory tusks — actually overgrown canine teeth — which are used for fighting and for digging clams out of the ocean floor. The biggest of the walrus bulls boast tusks that extend for three feet and weigh as much as nine pounds.

A walrus-tusk carving done by an Eskimo in the early 20th Century depicts both mythical and real animals. Ivory working, one of the oldest of crafts, was practiced 30,000 years ago by Stone Age carvers of tusks from mammoths.

the gravel from stream-bed depressions where gemstones are apt to collect because they are usually heavier than other minerals. Other areas can present more of a challenge. The excellent blue, green and black star sapphires of Bang Kha Cha, Thailand, for instance, are buried in the mud of tidal flats in the Gulf of Siam; miners must go out in boats at low tide, dredge up the gem-bearing mud and take it ashore to be washed in rattan sieves. Yet with a few variations, by far the most common method of mining for colored gemstones is one that Sri Lankans have been using for centuries. The only improvements brought to these operations by modern technology are the small gasoline-powered water pumps, often jerry-built affairs attached to old automobile engines, employed to remove water from the pits.

Sri Lankan prospectors sometimes seek out worthwhile sites with long metal rods, which are plunged into soft ground until they grate into the gem-bearing gravel below the surface. After a likely spot is located, workers dig a pit to depths ranging from three to 40 feet and shore up its sides with timbers. Miners slosh about filling cane baskets with gravel and soil. Meanwhile families, curious children and even casual passersby gather around the deepening pit to await, with eager anticipation, the discovery of a gemstone that will make the miners their fortune.

Once the oozy gravel is removed from the pit, it is taken to a nearby stream, where it is washed and swirled in round, shallow baskets called *watti*. The process requires a certain skill, since the *watti* must be manipulated in such a way as to eject lighter materials and concentrate the heavier gemstones in the bottom of the basket. When the swirling is finished, the remaining *dullam*, as washed gravel is called, is carefully sorted and inspected. "You never know," says one mine proprietor, "but the fact is there's nearly always something. If not alexandrite and the better stones, at least some garnets or topazes."

Whatever the residue of the *watti* reveals, it is almost sure to be disappointing at first glance. Converting the dull, misshapen stones found there into the brilliant gems that are the stuff of legends is the mission entrusted to the lapidary.

Named for the Greek word *"lapis,"* or "stone," the lapidaries who fashion colored gems concern themselves primarily with the play of light on color. The art requires an understanding of optics and is considerably more subtle than that of diamond cutting; the atomic arrangement in some gemstones, including emerald, is such that there are virtually no natural cutting lines.

Perhaps the first standard cutting form was the cabochon (to the ancients, the word "carbuncle" meant a red garnet cut in cabochon), with a flat back and a rounded convex top. Probably during the Middle Ages, some inspired artisan came up with the idea of cutting transparent gemstones, including diamonds, with their upper surfaces covered by small, flat faces, or facets. These imparted sparkle to any reasonably clear stone with a relatively high refractive index. From there, it was a short step to faceting the bottoms as well as the tops, so that the underside faces reflected light back up through the stones.

Today, because the cabochon displays color nicely but does little to enhance the play of light, it is mostly used for such opaque gemstones as agate, jade or moonstone. For clear or pale crystals, the so-called brilliant cut is by far the most popular, while a step cut — also known as the emerald

cut because it has been used for that gemstone for at least three centuries — is favored for darker colored gems.

For the lapidary, the brilliant and step cuts pose different problems and offer opposing advantages. The step cut, with its more or less rectangular facets, is considerably less complicated, but because the surface area of each facet is larger, it may require more time to grind and polish. Moreover, the step is cut more steeply, resulting in a thicker jewel, much of which may be concealed when it is mounted. The brilliant cut, on the other hand, has a multitude of tiny triangular facets, each of which must be painstakingly fashioned in a time-consuming process. When completed, however, the glitter it gives off goes far to disguise any cutting mistakes, while in the step cut errors are obvious.

In the Far East, the lapidary art is often a family industry, with techniques passed on from generation to generation; the tools are no more sophisticated than bamboo sticks to which gemstones are pasted to be ground against hand-cranked abrasive wheels that have not changed for centuries. Yet even in the modern shops of the West, lapidary principles remain much the same.

On examining a gemstone, the lapidary's first task is to calculate how best to bring out its color — one rule of thumb is that the crown of a dark stone should display the palest part of the crystal, but should emphasize the darkest aspect of a light gem. Once the crucial decisions are made, surplus material may be trimmed from the stone with an exact strike from a small hammer or with a saw — actually a steel disk with crushed diamond embedded in its rim.

Next, with the stone held in the lapidary's fingers, the crystal is pressed against a vertically rotating electric wheel whose surface is impregnated with an abrasive such as sand, garnet, emery or, most satisfactory of all, silicon carbide, a compound produced by heating sand and coke in electric

A tattooed opal miner shovels rubble from his private pit in the California desert. Too fragile for large-scale, mechanized mining, opal is generally gleaned with hand tools by miners working singly on small claims.

96

ovens. By now, the stone is beginning to assume its final shape — but to achieve perfection, something steadier than the human hand is necessary. In a process known as lapping, the stone is cemented to one end of a pencil-sized wooden stick called a dop stick. The other end of the stick is inserted into a hole in a "jamb peg," which nestles against the side of a horizontal grinding wheel, and the final faceting touches are made by adjusting the angle of the dop stick.

Polishing is the final and, surprisingly, the most hazardous phase of fashioning gemstones. Still attached to a dop stick in a jamb peg, the gemstone is pressed hard against a wheel charged with one of a wide variety of polishing powders and spinning at high speed. The stone, overheated by friction, may very well fracture. But if the operation is successful, the surface of the stone actually flows, spreading out in an extremely thin, transparent layer — and imparting to the gem a glorious shine.

Whether it remains in rough form or has succumbed to the skills of a lapidary, whether it is sold by a smuggler or a respectable merchant, whether it comes from the Far East, East Africa or South America, a costly colored gemstone is likely to pass through the hands of a middleman. That function is fulfilled by the international traders who operate from bases in such cities as New York, Paris, London, Amsterdam, Tokyo and Bombay and travel by plane, by limousine or by jeep, astride mules or on foot, to all the remote corners of the earth where beautiful crystals may be acquired.

Success in their chancy calling requires a knowledge of cultures and customs. In Thailand, the trader must always remember to remove his shoes before entering a merchant's home or office for a haggling session. "They feel the feet are a direct link with the soul," a New Yorker explains, "and, in a symbolic way, you are leaving the dirt of the world outside their doors." In Sri Lanka, tea is the ritual drink of gem trading, but in some other Far Eastern places it has been replaced, oddly enough, by Pepsi-Cola.

Trading techniques also differ greatly. In many parts of the world, the best of the bargain seems to be earned by whoever can achieve the highest decibel count. But in Sri Lanka, transactions are negotiated in silence. The seller and buyer join hands under a cloth. Each joint of each finger represents a price amount, and the bargaining is carried out by a process of joint-squeezing. Meanwhile, even though they cannot see what is happening beneath the cloth, spectators gather around to offer advice.

The general principles that govern value are of course a necessary part of the trader's store of knowledge, and an understanding of such erudite subjects as specific gravity is mandatory. Most colored gemstones are sold by weight, with the number of carats expressed to two decimal places. Thus, an emerald described as a "seven point two two" would weigh 7.22 carats. Within a certain range, perhaps between a half carat and five carats, value increases sharply with weight. Beyond that, because the stone may be too large to be worn comfortably, the value curve begins to level off.

The successful trader must combine an appraiser's skills with a policeman's innate suspicion. He must, among many other things, understand that although a colored gemstone may be relatively "clean" — that is, free from inclusions or other flaws — it may nevertheless lack the glow or fire that makes others of its kind more attractive. He must therefore be able to

A crystal of kunzite five and a quarter inches high displays the delicate hue that quickly elevated the mineral to gem status after its discovery in 1902. The richer color concentrated at the ends of the crystal is the result of an optical peculiarity of kunzite: The light that passes through the length of the crystal emerges more strongly colored than the light that traverses the gemstone from side to side.

distinguish, in a descending order of desirability, between the stone which has "life" and those which are "tired," or "sleepy" or, alas, "dead."

Even when buying from someone he knows and trusts, a trader can be tricked by the gemstones themselves. Nearly all colored crystals change in appearance according to lighting conditions; the ruby that appears to burn with an inner fire beneath a tropical sun may be lifeless in the artificial lights of a Paris salon. For the purpose of making comparisons, many traders carry sets of gems with established quality in normal lighting. Some simply wear rings set with a ruby, a sapphire and an emerald, each with acceptable characteristics.

A gem's appearance may have been enhanced by heating, a process that has become so widely practiced — 95 per cent of the rubies and sapphires that come from the Far East have been heat-treated — and so consistently successful that it is no longer regarded as a deception. While there is an element of risk (a ruby, for instance, may be dulled by one application of heat only to have its value multiplied by another), the rewards are prodigious: A milky-white sapphire from Bangkok may be transformed into a beautiful, clear blue; yellowish Brazilian aquamarine becomes the most-prized shade of blue; and amethyst acquires the yellowish brown shade much desired as citrine.

But the gemstone buyer can be the target of endless other forms of chicanery. Although no professional trader would be fooled by the plastic-coated quartz that is sometimes sold to tourists in Colombia as emerald, it takes a practiced eye to detect an assembled stone — in which a layer of fine stone has been superimposed on a poor one — or a green crystal in which minute surface cracks have been healed, temporarily, by soaking in warm oil. One expert Manhattan dealer was bilked out of several hundred thousands of dollars on a batch of Zambian emeralds. "The oiling process had done such a marvelous job," he ruefully recalls. "About nine months after these emeralds were purchased, the oil dried out, leaving their flaws and imperfections extremely visible."

In their personalities and appearances, and even in their tastes for species of colored gemstones, the traders vary vastly. Yet, like all those in this fascinating business, they have a common denominator in their love of the products for which they risk their fortunes and sometimes their lives. As gemologist Joel Arem put it: "There is nothing on earth that can begin to match the breathtaking beauty of a gemstone that has both a strong body color and a strong dispersion, or play of color, that comes out of a well-cut stone like a spectral blaze. Natural colors are more subtle and lovely than any man has been able to create." Ω

A DEADLY QUEST FOR EMERALDS

In Colombia's lush green Muzo valley region, where the hills are riddled with veins of calcite bearing the world's finest emeralds, outlaw mining is endemic. Some 15,000 *guaqueros,* the Spanish term for "treasure hunters," steal from Muzo's several emerald mines (and from each other) in an endless and often bloody quest for instant riches.

So lucrative is this predatory profession that the Colombian government cannot control it; in 1973 more than 900 *guaqueros* were murdered in conflicts over Muzo's emerald bounty, and the government had to shut down the mines, which had operated sporadically since the 17th Century. Three years later, private companies leased the mines from the government, which then circled Muzo with National Police to safeguard its share of the bounty. Yet the police, whether because of payoffs or sympathy for the *guaqueros,* make only occasional arrests.

The police do prevent illicit forays into the mines by day, so the *guaqueros* spend the daylight hours sifting for gems in the bed of the Río Itoco, which carries rubble loosened by the blasting and excavating done at the mines. By night, however, men, women and even children dig individual tunnels, known as mouseholes, sometimes for hundreds of feet, into the company mines. Cave-ins and asphyxiation kill many *guaqueros* each year.

A *guaquero* who finds an emerald, and successfully conceals it from rivals, will sell it to one of the emerald dealers, called *esmeralderos,* who cluster around the Río Itoco. An *esmeraldero,* in turn, can sell a stone for far more than his purchase price, but he must first get the gem to Bogotá, a six-hour journey along a road where robbery and murder are a constant threat.

Emerald poachers gather after a night of clandestine digging in a mine in Colombia's Muzo valley. The hills behind them contain the world's richest emerald deposits.

While mining company bulldozers expose the veins of emerald-bearing calcite that streak Muzo's shale mountains, scavengers throng the Río Itoco

below. The rubble, which often contains emeralds that have been overlooked, is pushed into the riverbed.

Guaqueros by the thousands scour the bed of the Río Itoco in their search for emeralds, rummaging through coarse mining slag that has already been

sifted by countless others. A fortunate scavenger may uncover one emerald a year

In constant danger of suffocation, cave-in and discovery by police, a *guaquero* scrapes the walls of a tunnel he has dug into an emerald-bearing vein. About 2,000 such tunnels, some as much as 200 yards long, honeycomb the Muzo hills.

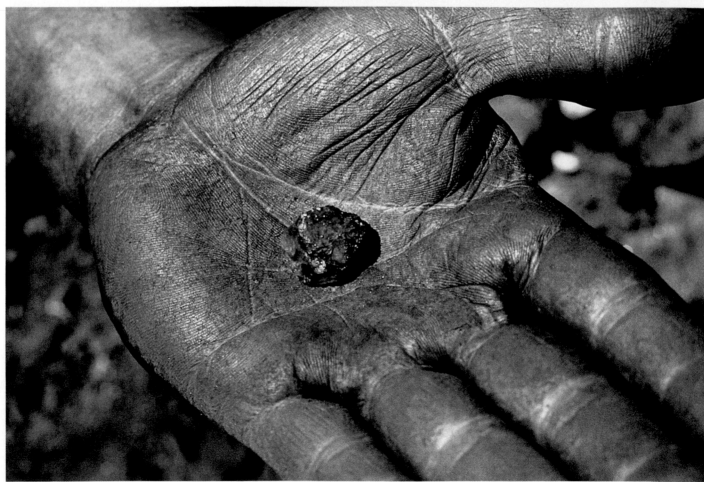

A *guaquero* displays a glittering emerald in a hand blackened by digging in carboniferous shale.

A National Police patrol leads away some *guaqueros* arrested for illegal mining. Such arrests are infrequent and jail sentences are generally short.

A protective revolver lies nearby as a cluster of illicit emeralds passes through one more pair of hands on its way to fashionable jewelry stores.

The end of the quest: Candles flicker beside the body of a *guaquero* killed by guards patrolling the mines.

Chapter 4

BUILDING A DIAMOND EMPIRE

It was a fine December day in 1866, and 15-year-old Erasmus Jacobs had taken a break from his chores on his father's farm in South Africa. Resting against a tree on the banks of the Orange River, young Jacobs was attracted by a pebble glinting brightly in the sunlight. Thinking his little sister might like to play with the sparkling stone, he scooped it up, took it home and unwittingly started a chain of economic, political and social upheavals that has continued to this day.

When a family friend named Schalk van Niekerk, who knew a bit about gems, expressed an interest in the stone, Erasmus' mother insisted on giving it to him. The glittering pebble aroused great interest and hot dispute in the nearby town of Colesberg; one self-styled expert bet a new hat that it was a relatively worthless topaz. But it was soon confirmed that the stone was in fact a 21-carat diamond, eventually to be called the Eureka. It sold for £500, five times the cost of a comfortable house in England; accounts differ as to whether the Jacobs family realized anything from the sale.

Even if he did not profit from it, Erasmus Jacobs had delivered to the world the first of a deluge of diamonds that would soon begin flowing from South Africa. Throughout history, diamonds had been something everyone had heard about but few had ever seen, let alone possessed. The diamonds of antiquity, most of which had been found in India, had accumulated in the collections of a few mighty princes. After diamonds were discovered in the jungles of Brazil in 1725, the world's supply had increased considerably; where it had taken India 20 centuries to produce 12 million carats of diamonds, Brazil's riverbeds yielded about 16 million carats in a century and a half. But diamonds were still available only to the very wealthy.

South Africa would change all that. Within a decade of Erasmus Jacobs' find, South Africa's mines would have yielded more diamonds than those of Brazil, and within another decade they would be disgorging three million carats in a single year to an avid, worldwide, mass market; the diamond would be everyone's gemstone. More astonishing still, by 1889 virtually their entire production would be passing through the hands of an enigmatic, power-hungry Englishman named Cecil John Rhodes.

When Cecil Rhodes first set foot in Africa in 1870, he possessed no towering ambitions. He was a frail and distant youth of 17, the son of a Hertfordshire vicar. He had been shipped off to the Natal district on the eastern coast of South Africa to join an older brother, Herbert, who had settled there in the false hope of becoming a country gentleman and a cotton farmer. The plan was for the young man to improve his health — he would

Empire builder and master of the diamond cartel, Cecil Rhodes is portrayed as a colossus standing astride Africa by *Punch* in 1892, at the peak of his power. "The vastness of his frame," wrote one historian, "was matched by the breadth of his vision."

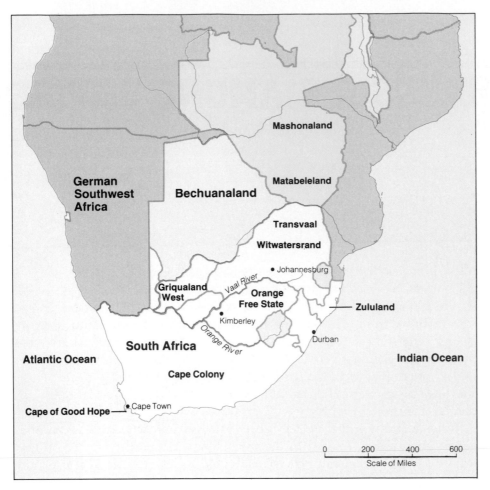

Map labels: Mashonaland, German Southwest Africa, Bechuanaland, Matabeleland, Transvaal, Witwatersrand, Johannesburg, Vaal River, Griqualand West, Orange Free State, Zululand, Kimberley, Orange River, Durban, South Africa, Atlantic Ocean, Indian Ocean, Cape Colony, Cape of Good Hope, Cape Town

0   200   400   600
Scale of Miles

When diamonds were discovered there in the last third of the 19th Century, South Africa consisted of a collection of sparsely populated tribal lands, British colonies and two republics, the Transvaal and the Orange Free State. The republics were founded by Boer farmers who had trekked inland to avoid British rule.

suffer all his life from a weak heart — and earn enough money to pay for his education in England at Oxford University. Rhodes landed at Durban, about 800 miles northeast of the Cape of Good Hope. He was met not by his brother but by a neighbor who reported that Herbert Rhodes had been caught up in the wild diamond fever then sweeping South Africa.

Although the Eureka find had been reported in the Colesberg newspaper as "The Wonderful South African Diamond," it had not attracted widespread attention. Not so the next diamond discovery, which, amazingly enough, also had come into the hands of Schalk van Niekerk. In 1868 a young Griqua tribesman named Swartboy had come across a large glassy stone near the Orange River. According to one story, Swartboy offered the stone to a farmer in exchange for a night's lodging and was turned away. "Go to Schalk van Niekerk," said the farmer. "He likes stones. I don't."

Van Niekerk, who lived close by, immediately bought the stone, bestowing on the amazed Swartboy as payment every head of livestock on his farm — 500 sheep, 10 cows and a horse. When the 83.5-carat stone — later named the Star of South Africa — fetched a price of £11,200, the world suddenly took notice. In a matter of weeks, thousands of men from Great Britain, the Dominions, the United States and elsewhere began to pour into the country, bound for the banks of the Orange and Vaal Rivers in search of diamonds. Among them, in the summer of 1870, was Herbert Rhodes.

Prospectors arriving at Cape Town and other ports had to trek inland as far as 600 miles to reach the diggings. The trip took at least 40 days by oxcart, but many could not afford that comparative luxury and had to walk the whole way to the muddy, crowded, chaotic and malaria-ridden camptowns lining the two rivers. The prospectors, many of whom had never done any sort of mining before, staked out plots of about 30 feet to a side

Elegant and aloof, Cecil Rhodes at the age of 24 had already become a major owner of the fabulous De Beers diamond mine in South Africa. Rudyard Kipling later called him "the greatest of living men."

and started shoveling away the top layer of dirt, looking for the gravel in which the diamonds might be found. They washed away the earth, using a rudimentary recovery method that came to be referred to as wet digging, and dumped the remaining gravel out on a table to examine the load pebble by pebble, picking out the precious stones.

Food was expensive and scarce; shelter was improvised with canvas and corrugated iron; and frustrations were endless. Yet the occasional bonanza kept the frenzied prospectors at their backbreaking labors. After working for six months without finding anything, one Englishman gave his claim away and left. The next day his successor found a fine 29.5-carat diamond. Such stories, told and retold in the camps, kept the men in agonies of indecision: Should they dig a little deeper or move on a little farther?

The luckless Herbert Rhodes did not strike it rich in the summer of 1870; he soon returned to his farm near Durban and with Cecil's help set out his cotton. But the novice farmers placed the plants too close together and the crop failed. The outcome confirmed what anyone who saw Cecil Rhodes during that time must have thought — that he was a highly unlikely cotton farmer. He went about the rough frontier community in ill-fitting, ever more tattered schoolboy slacks and blazer, and in preparation for Oxford he spent his spare time dutifully laboring over a set of Greek and Latin texts. He was subject to violent outbursts of temper and sometimes sank into a total silence that would last for days on end.

Meanwhile, at about the time Herbert Rhodes joined the hordes of prospectors sifting the mud of the Vaal River, a man known to history only by the name of Bam found another diamond in a field 60 miles from the nearest river diggings. The experience of the diamond prospectors — some of whom were veterans of the California Gold Rush — had taught them that precious things such as gold and gems were to be found in riverbeds. It would become clear only later that the stones along the riverbanks did not originate there but had been carried from elsewhere by water. Bam's discovery, far from being an anomaly, was in fact a major step closer to the primary source of all South African diamonds.

Those who followed Bam's lead and went inland to dig were left for a time to their own devices by most of the miners. But the growing number of good stones inland soon provoked a new rush of miners who quickly followed up on any new find, moving from one farm to the next whenever a big stone was discovered. The diggers still did not realize that they were now scratching the ground near the spot where many of the diamonds found along the Orange River probably first emerged on the earth's surface.

In 1871 a man named Fleetwood Rawstorne staked out a claim on a farm in the promising inland area, between the Orange and Vaal Rivers and east of their confluence. Rawstorne did not prosper; he gambled away his first claim and found little more than a single two-carat diamond on a later site. The two brothers who owned the farm were no happier with their luck, but for different reasons. Straitlaced Boers — descendants of the early Dutch settlers of South Africa — they had no interest in prospecting and were overwhelmed by the rush of prospectors who swarmed in from nearby diggings, tearing up the land in a frantic search for diamonds. To make the best of a hopeless situation, the brothers sold the farm (which they had purchased for £50 eleven years earlier) to a mining syndicate for £6,300 and moved on in search of peace and quiet. In so doing, Johannes and Diedrich de Beer unwittingly gave up a pair of fabulously rich diamond deposits, one of which — the one where Fleetwood Rawstorne had made his meager find — would become the site of the illustrious Kimberley mine; equally unwittingly, they won immortality for their family name.

In May of 1871 the call of the inland diggings took Herbert Rhodes off prospecting again, while Cecil stayed behind to bring in that year's cotton. Although they had learned from the previous year's failure and this time the yield was good, prices were depressed, and in October he abandoned the farm and set out for Herbert's claims — three of them, each measuring 31 by 31 feet — at what was now known as the Kimberley mine.

Conditions around the new town of Kimberley were even more chaotic and primitive than at the river diggings. A dusty jumble of tents and iron shacks housed claims offices, law offices, banks, diamond-buying shops, saloons, brothels, gambling dens and a church or two. The town's motley collection of diamond-rush characters was constantly in motion, for it

When their land became the site of a diamond rush in 1871, the taciturn farmer Johannes de Beer (*above*) and his brother Diedrich sold out and moved to more tranquil environs.

seemed to them that the waste of even a few minutes might cost the finding of a great stone. Nearby farms supplied the town's food and firewood, but manufactured goods had to be hauled in by wagon from the coast.

The miners, many of whom had rushed to Kimberley from the Orange and Vaal diggings, staked out their claims and started mining much as they had on the river. The main difference was that there was no water to wash the dirt from the pebbles; the ground had to be broken up by hand, and the mines in this area thus came to be called dry diggings. As Cecil Rhodes later observed, at first sight the mines looked "like an immense number of antheaps covered with black ants, as thick as can be, the latter represented by human beings." If Rhodes was taken aback by the appearance of Kimberley, the miners who met him were no less confounded by this odd newcomer who, at the age of 18, had taken it upon himself to manage Herbert's claims. Soon, though, the mercurial Herbert headed north on a new quest, this time for gold, selling his diggings to his younger brother — who quick-

At one Kimberley mine, where water is scarce, diamond seekers in the 1870s employ a process called dry digging. African workers sifted the earth dug from the claims through rough sieves; sorters (*seated at center*) then carefully picked through it by hand to find the gems.

ly proved that he could hold his own in a rough-and-ready enterprise.

Kimberley miners used local tribesmen to do the digging, but few of the claim holders, it developed, could manage black laborers as efficiently as Rhodes. He had brought his own team of Zulu workers from his farm, and although these proud warriors held paid labor in low esteem they felt honor-bound to work hard to repay money Rhodes had lent them. Furthermore, few miners could gauge the worth of a stone as shrewdly as Rhodes; "I am averaging £100 per week," he wrote his mother in late 1871, and in less than two years in the diamond fields he had amassed £10,000. At that point he confounded his fellow miners again by putting his claims in the hands of a trusted acquaintance, Charles Rudd, and sailing for England — bearing a small fortune in diamonds in the pockets of his tattered clothing — to enter Oxford. There, snubbed by fellow students who were put off by his tall tales of Africa, Rhodes took refuge in a deepening moroseness and arrogance.

But a feeling of his own innate authority deepened as well, and before long he was overcome by a strong sense of purpose. He was an early convert to social Darwinism — which held that elite classes possessed inherent biological superiority. He concluded that the fittest were meant not only to survive but to lead. And he listened raptly as social theorist John Ruskin challenged undergraduates to fulfill England's destiny. "This is what England must either do or perish," Ruskin exhorted. "She must found colonies as far and as fast as she is able, formed of her most energetic and worthiest men." This dream of a worldwide British Empire, engendered in those heady student days, was the inspiration for a mystical sense of mission that drove Rhodes to go after the whole South African diamond trade as a means of bringing southern Africa under the sway of Anglo-Saxon civilization. "If there be a God," he once told some friends at Oxford, "I think that what He would like me to do is paint as much of Africa British red as possible."

During the next eight years Rhodes worked doggedly toward his bachelor of arts degree, his studies interrupted repeatedly by the need to return to Africa, either for his health or to deal with some situation in his mines. It was during these African interludes that Rhodes began acquiring immense wealth and power in the mines, aided by a number of events that coincided to end forever the anarchy that held sway at Kimberley while thousands of miners feverishly worked their individual claims.

Despite the enormous quantities of diamonds reaching the world market from South Africa — more than a million carats between 1872 and 1874 — prices remained stable for a time. But a worldwide financial panic in 1873 sent the diamond market into a slow but steady decline, just as the claim holders were finding it more difficult and more costly to extract their gems. Early miners around Kimberley found their stones in "yellow ground," weathered rock of a type later named kimberlite. When they reached the bottom of the soft yellow ground and struck the "blue ground" that lay underneath, many miners thought their claims had petered out. But Rhodes, having consulted the few geologists in the area, suspected that the blue ground was very likely as rich in diamonds as the yellow.

As events would soon confirm and geologists would soon understand, he was right. In fact the yellow ground was merely the uppermost layer of deep, carrot-shaped pipes of diamond-bearing rock that had been formed by ancient volcanoes. The blue ground was simply hard kimberlite that had not yet been broken down or discolored by weathering.

The Geology of African Diamonds

Flowing west for 1,300 miles through the heart of southern Africa, the Orange River is the central feature of a region that contains in unique abundance the three kinds of geologic locations where almost all diamonds are found.

The primary sources of the precious crystals are the pipes of volcanic rock called kimberlite that erupted to the surface of South Africa's inland plateau between 70 and 150 million years ago. During the eons that followed, the erosive forces of nature leveled the volcanoes and carried tons of exposed kimberlite to the upper reaches of the Orange and such tributary rivers as the Vaal.

Washed downstream, some of the diamond-bearing alluvium came to rest on the river's bottom. The remainder was carried all the way to the South Atlantic, where powerful currents swept some of the stones as far as 50 miles up the coast before depositing them on the rocky terraces that formed the shore.

Rhodes also realized that the Kimberley, De Beers and other pipes could not be mined indefinitely from the surface down, with the so-called open-pit method. When the digging started at the Kimberley pipe, the hundreds of claim holders had cooperated to the extent of leaving widths of unexcavated earth along the edges of their claims. Their neighbors would do the same, thus creating roadways and walls between the claims; the understanding was that the diggers would break up and mine the intact earth later, when it was time to reestablish the roads and walls at a lower level.

Each miner tended to dig at his own pace, however, so the convenient moments for tearing down the barriers were often missed. Roads and walls began to crumble and cave in on the claims, and sometimes on the miners. After touring the Kimberley pipe, the English novelist Anthony Trollope said it was as if "some diabolically ingenious architect had contrived a house with 500 rooms, not one of which should be on the same floor, and to and from none of which there should be a pair of stairs or a door or a window."

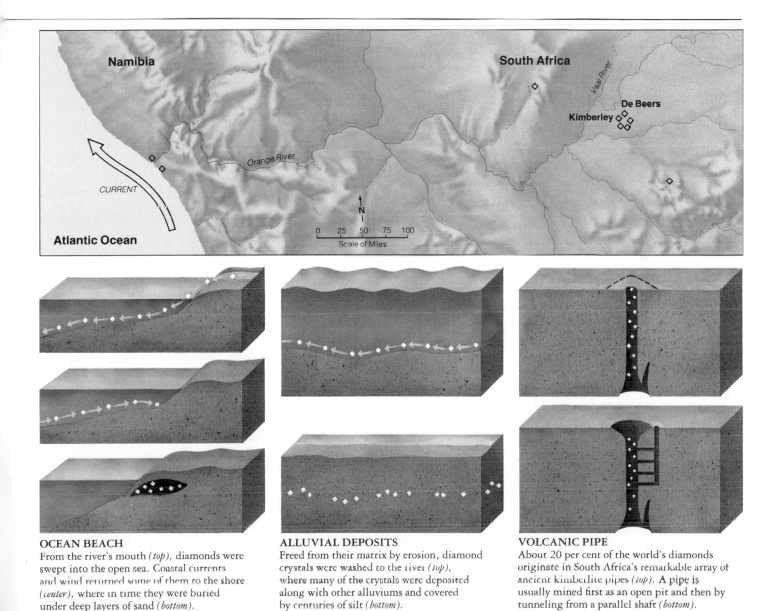

OCEAN BEACH
From the river's mouth (top), diamonds were swept into the open sea. Coastal currents and wind returned some of them to the shore (center), where in time they were buried under deep layers of sand (bottom).

ALLUVIAL DEPOSITS
Freed from their matrix by erosion, diamond crystals were washed to the river (top), where many of the crystals were deposited along with other alluviums and covered by centuries of silt (bottom).

VOLCANIC PIPE
About 20 per cent of the world's diamonds originate in South Africa's remarkable array of ancient kimberlite pipes (top). A pipe is usually mined first as an open pit and then by tunneling from a parallel shaft (bottom).

Furthermore, the mining surface in the pipe, for all its variations in depth, was moving inexorably downward. Roadways descending into the deepening hole, even those that were wide and well shored up, became too steep to negotiate safely. Soon the miners had to string wire ropes from the rim of the hole down to each claim; along these cables ran open cars carrying workers and kimberlite. Before long the pipe was crisscrossed with a chaotic webbing of rusting cables running in all directions and slowing the progress of the cars. Along with these difficulties, the miners were dogged by severe flooding, a product of the area's infrequent but torrential rains and seeping groundwater (for a time, Rhodes ran a modestly successful pumping business with machines laboriously hauled in from the coast).

Worried or bankrupt claim holders were giving up on all sides, but Rhodes, undaunted by the low diamond prices and the unproven value of the blue ground, began buying up claims — mostly in the De Beers pipe — as quickly as he could scrape together the money. He had perceived opportunity where most diggers saw only a steadily worsening situation: If the numerous claims in the small open-pit mines could be consolidated, capital could be accumulated and financing arranged for large-scale mining and extracting operations. He organized his growing holdings into a joint-stock company, memorializing the luckless brothers Johannes and Diedrich by naming it the De Beers Mining Company, Limited.

Rhodes's status in Kimberley was growing, along with his reputation for eccentricity. He had a way of breaking his long silences with sudden, passionate monologues that seized the attention of everyone within earshot. He

For a fee of 10 shillings, this renewable license issued by British colonial authorities in 1871 granted a digger rights for one month to a claim 30 feet square, or — as the diggers put it — "10 times the size of your grave." A claim could be taken over by another miner if the license holder failed to work it for eight days.

A fleet of oxcarts fills Kimberley's market square in the 1880s after a six-week, 600-mile supply journey from the coast. Everything the mining town needed to survive, including timber for housing and for propping up the mine walls, was delivered on these clumsy wagons.

once startled a group of miners by shouting: "You think I am keen about money. I assure you I wouldn't care a damn if I lost all I have tomorrow. It's the game I like." And the scope of his game was becoming clear. He meant to become the unquestioned master of South African diamond mining.

Rhodes had supreme confidence in his ability to judge, sway and direct other men. He now used that talent to gain an important ally, a diminutive German named Alfred Beit, who had arrived in Kimberley as the agent of a Hamburg diamond-buying firm. Beit had learned the diamond trade during a five-year apprenticeship with a firm of diamond merchants in Amsterdam. He possessed almost total recall and could recognize individual stones years after they had passed through his hands. Equally important, he understood finance and was welcome in both the London and Paris branches of the House of Rothschild, the powerful international banking concern.

One evening in 1879 Rhodes struck up a conversation with Beit, whom he knew slightly. Before long Beit stated flatly, "I am going to control the whole diamond output before I am much older."

"I have made up my mind to do the same," replied Rhodes. "We had better join hands." The impromptu overture was one of Rhodes's wisest moves. Beit not only brought to the partnership his expertise in the financial and diamond markets and his contacts with European banks, but served Rhodes personally as a loyal critic and friend.

Rhodes needed such a friend. In the rough-and-tumble male fraternity of the Kimberley miners his aloof demeanor was making him increasingly unpopular, and he was especially suspect because he conspicuously shunned women. Rhodes was the subject of many a salacious rumor, particularly after he changed his will in favor of his private secretary, a young man named Neville Pickering (who, as it happened, died shortly thereafter). Later in life, when Queen Victoria questioned him about his apparent dislike of females, he cleverly replied that he could have no ill feeling toward the sex of which Her Majesty was a member. Still, his attitude did not do anything to ease his relationships with his colleagues in the mines, nor did his continuing accumulation of other men's claims.

Rhodes was not the only man buying up diggings in Kimberley. Indeed, for all his towering ambitions he was far from the biggest operator. No one profited so ostentatiously from the merger process — or constituted so formidable an obstacle to Rhodes's feverish designs — as a boisterous little Cockney promoter named Barney Barnato. Born Barnett Isaacs, Barnato began his commercial career as a 14-year-old boy selling goods from a pushcart in London's East End. He soon found more varied employment, working as a music-hall entertainer and later as a prize fighter. At the age of 18, bent on riches, he invested his meager capital in 60 boxes of low-grade cigars and a steerage ticket to South Africa. Bad as they were, the cigars brought a good price in Kimberley. With the profits Barnato bought a pony and an old buggy and became a *kopje walloper* — an itinerant diamond trader — winning friends among the miners by regaling them with an inexhaustible supply of off-color stories as he wandered from claim to claim.

Barnato was nearly illiterate, but he was tough, entertaining and shrewd, and he soon improved his business by renting office space at a bar patronized by diggers. He was a man of his word and did his best to deal fairly with others, but he let no man wrong him without retaliating. "If you are going to fight," he often said, "get in the first blow."

Like Rhodes, Barnato believed in the worth of blue ground, and in 1876 he spent £3,000 for four claims at the heart of the Kimberley mine. Soon they were yielding an average of £1,800 worth of diamonds a week. He sold shares in his enterprise, eventually named the Kimberley Central Diamond Mining Company, to European investors, and bought more and more claims around his original parcel. He hired a large labor crew and housed it in nearby compounds; he created a private police force to control theft and smuggling, and sank the first deep shaft into the Kimberley mine.

By 1885, Barnato was making £200,000 a year — four times as much as Rhodes — and he let no one doubt his lofty new status. He built a house in an exclusive quarter of Kimberley, went about in a coach-and-four and wore loud but expensive suits. As his wealth grew, his popularity declined somewhat among envious miners, but in his role of king of the Kimberley mine, Barnato remained as friendly and jocular as he had been as a *kopje walloper.*

As the biggest shareholder in the Kimberley mine, a much richer pipe than Rhodes's De Beers mine, Barnato stood squarely in the way of the only prize in Cecil Rhodes's game — total control. Rhodes was nevertheless confident of winning, simply because he was certain that every man had his price. Rhodes's inherent cynicism on that score was powerfully confirmed when, in 1881, he won election to the Cape of Good Hope Colony Parliament by buying the requisite votes.

Although Barnato agreed with Rhodes on the need to consolidate the mines and control production, each intended to be the man in control. Barnato was also disposed to be uncooperative on another count; he knew

Hand-powered winches on crude platforms line the rim of the Big Hole at Kimberley in 1873. Hard "blue ground" was hauled in buckets from the claim sites hundreds of feet below, then carted off to level areas, called floors, to be pulverized and sifted for diamonds.

"Never has any eye seen such a marvellous show of mining as was given in this grand amphitheatre," exulted Gardner Williams, an American engineer who went to work at the Kimberley mine in 1887 as its general manager. The discovery that diamond-laden rock ran far deeper than suspected at Kimberley had set off a new frenzy of exploitation.

By 1874, the last of the crumbling roadways across the Big Hole at Kimberley had been broken up for their ore content. What remained was a huge oval pit, 1,000 feet long by 600 across. This "demon's cauldron," as Williams called it, grew deeper every day except Sunday, when the fortune seekers rested.

At about 80 feet the easily shoveled "yellow ground" gave way to hard, slate-blue rock that was equally rich in diamonds. The miners attacked this "blue ground," or kimberlite, with pick and shovel, loading it into rawhide buckets that were winched up the sheer walls of the pit.

Soon horses, then steam, supplanted the men at the winches. Steel cables replaced the hoisting ropes, and hide buckets gave way to tubs that could hold six cubic feet of diamond ore. But depth created new problems — and risks.

The ultimate threats were floods and cave-ins. With terrifying regularity the walls of the Big Hole crumbled and fell, burying claims and miners alike. By the 1890s, open mining in the demon's cauldron was all but abandoned in favor of a practical, if less spectacular, underground system of shafts and tunnels.

Horses yoked to horizontal wooden wheels called whims replace manpower for hauling ore out of the deepening mine in 1874. A year later, the first steam-powered winch was installed to replace horses.

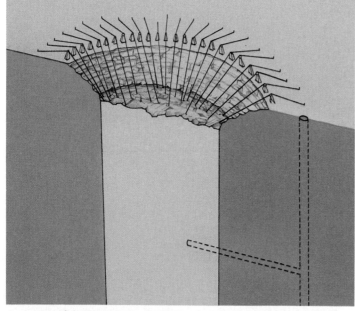

A cutaway of the Big Hole in the 1870s, the mine's rim lined with winches, shows the irregular bottom at 1,000 feet. The vertical pipe of kimberlite (*blue*) was sheathed by a funnel of barren ground, or reef, composed of soft basalt and shale. As digging progressed, the reef often collapsed, eventually requiring that separate shafts be sunk to reach the deeper ore by tunnel.

The honeycombed chasm at Kimberley
(*above*) is crisscrossed by a skein of cables,
the primary means of moving men and ore to
and from the floor of the mine (*right*).

that Rhodes held him in low esteem and had referred to him openly as "that cunning little Jew." Moreover, Barnato disdained what he and many others considered Rhodes's "crackpot" dreams of expanding the British Empire.

But Barnato had a weakness. Despite his wealth and his continued popularity with the ordinary diggers, another goal had eluded him — acceptance by Kimberley's nascent upper class of businessmen and government officials. He especially coveted the approval of one of Rhodes's closest allies, a young Scottish surgeon named Leander Starr Jameson who, as one of the few professional people in the area, was a leader of what passed for society in Kimberley. For his part, Jameson nursed an almost pathological contempt for Barnato and had snubbed him repeatedly in the streets of Kimberley. Rhodes shared a house with Jameson, and aware of the helpful effect it might have, invited Barnato to his home for a meeting. There, Rhodes laid his cards on the table: He intended, he said, to buy Barnato out.

However impressed Barnato may have been by his surroundings, he was far from being intimidated. Instead of naming a price for his Kimberley Central shares, he suggested with a serene smile that Rhodes might himself be swallowed up in the struggle for monopoly. Oddly, as the two men drew their battle lines, they began to warm to each other: Rhodes developed a grudging admiration for Barnato as "a tough nut to crack," and Barnato began to admire in Rhodes a combativeness much like his own.

His direct approach to Barnato repulsed, Rhodes took aim at the company with the next-largest holding in the Kimberley pipe — the Compagnie Française des Mines de Diamant du Cap de Bon Espérance, popularly known as the French Company. Rhodes made an offer to buy the company, but the alert Barnato immediately countered with a higher bid and made it clear that he would top any offer Rhodes made.

Stalemated again, Rhodes decided to try to buy Barnato off and invited him to another parley. According to one account the flamboyant Barnato, meaning to intimidate his rival, brought along a suitcase brimming with more than a million pounds' worth of Kimberley Central's biggest, finest diamonds, neatly packeted according to size and quality. Unfazed, Rhodes demanded that Barnato name a price for ending his opposition to Rhodes's purchase of the French Company. Barnato refused. Another stalemate.

Rhodes then made a surprising new offer: If Barnato would stand aside and let him buy the French Company under the terms of his original offer, he would immediately sell it to Barnato — for an equivalent amount of Kimberley Central stock. It was a brilliant countermove. Denied the opportunity to increase his holdings directly, Rhodes was proposing to increase his influence in an enlarged Kimberley Central empire. And Barnato, despite the risk of letting Rhodes into an influential position in Kimberley Central, could not pass up the chance to get the French Company without spending a penny. Barnato agreed to Rhodes's proposition on the spot.

Having concluded what he thought was a winning deal, the ebullient Barnato began showing Rhodes the fortune in gems he had carried to the meeting. While opening packet after packet, Rhodes suddenly realized that the fortune in stones before him was not a mere sampling of Kimberley Central's inventory, but the cream of its inventory. Rhodes was inspired. "Barney," he said, "have you ever seen a bucketful of diamonds? It has always been a dream of mine to see a bucketful of diamonds." Rhodes called for a bucket and before Barnato realized what was happening began spilling

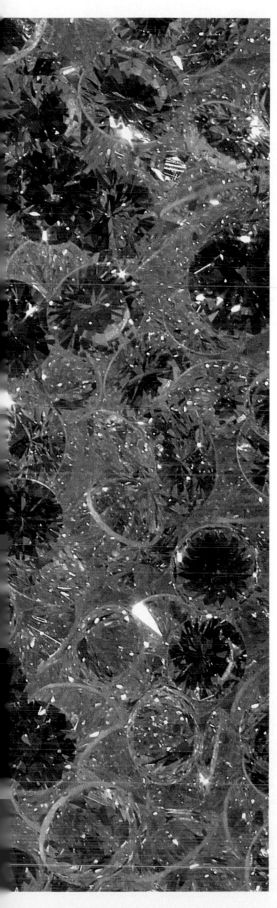

the glittering stones from their wrappings. The pile rose, eventually, almost to the brim of the bucket. The seemingly entranced Rhodes dug his hands into the stones and stirred them as Barnato watched with pride.

"A good show, isn't it?" said Barnato. "Could De Beers do as much?"

"No," Rhodes answered, "De Beers could never have done it."

Filling the bucket with diamonds, far from being the impulsive act of an eccentric, was in fact a masterly maneuver. With the deal completed for a sizable portion of Kimberley Central shares, Rhodes intended to go after every additional share that could be found until he had full control. He knew Barnato would bid against him at every step, so he made his first move in the share-buying battle with a few simple movements of his hands. Until the diamonds jumbled together in the bucket had been re-sorted and reclassified, a process that would take several weeks, they could not be sold; Rhodes had temporarily deprived Barnato of more than a million pounds' worth of capital.

With Barnato thus handcuffed, Rhodes sprang into action. In just a few weeks during February of 1888, backed by millions of pounds in loans obtained by his well-connected aide Alfred Beit from the House of Rothschild, Rhodes picked up enough shares of Kimberley Central to wrest control from Barnato.

Rhodes moved promptly to incorporate Kimberley Central into his De Beers Mining Company. Barnato, still a major shareholder in Kimberley Central, had no objections so long as his own position in the amalgamated organization was assured, but he dug his heels in over Rhodes's intention to make the new company a vehicle for colonial expansion. What, he asked, had a diamond-mining company to do with British imperialism? Finally, however, when Rhodes promised to give him the trappings of respectability — membership in the Kimberley Club and even a seat in the Cape Parliament — Barnato gave in. "You have a fancy for making an empire," Barnato told Rhodes. "Well, I suppose I must give it to you."

In short order Rhodes bought out the two remaining mines in the Kimberley area for about a million pounds apiece and became, in 1889, absolute dictator at last of 90 per cent of the world's production of diamonds. He acted at once to exercise his hard-won power.

Rhodes faced a situation previously unknown in the diamond market — the presence of more gems than even the expanding world demand could absorb. Prices had withstood the unprecedented flood of South African gems for a time because of a phenomenon upon which the diamond trade would rest thereafter — the emergence of prosperous industrial societies in France, Germany, Great Britain and, particularly, the United States. But the market had broken badly several times, and Rhodes knew that the relative price stability of the late 1880s was unlikely to continue.

His answer to the market's precariousness was to restrict all sales of De Beers diamonds to a group of 10 dealers who became known as the Diamond Syndicate. And according to one account he limited production through an even simpler device — all newly dug gems from the Kimberley mines were placed in a wooden box measuring two feet long by nine inches wide that was kept in a heavy safe at company headquarters. When the box was full, he shut down the mines.

Rhodes took steps, meanwhile, to combat smuggling and black marketeering of stolen gems, practices that had gone on since the beginning of

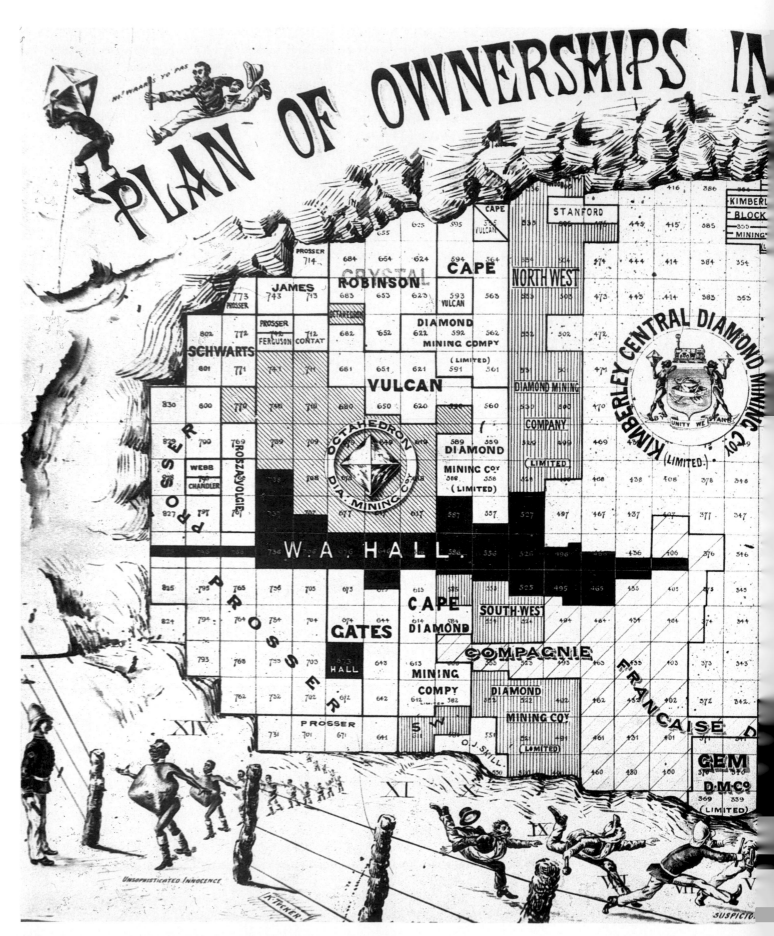

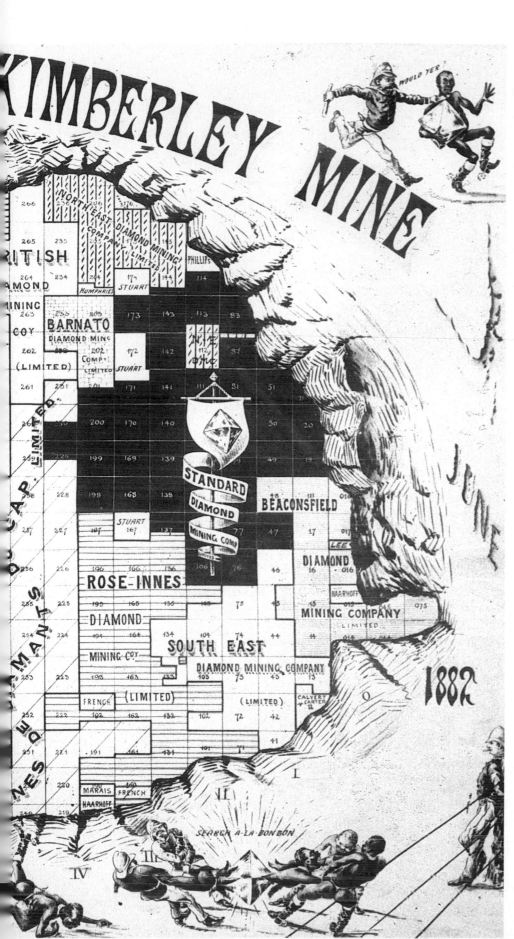

Attired in frock coat and wing collar, Barney Barnato, a onetime London street urchin, exudes confident respectability. Until he was bested by Cecil Rhodes in 1888, Barnato dominated diamond production at the Kimberley mine.

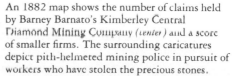

An 1882 map shows the number of claims held by Barney Barnato's Kimberley Central Diamond Mining Company (center) and a score of smaller firms. The surrounding caricatures depict pith-helmeted mining police in pursuit of workers who have stolen the precious stones.

African mining. Diggers were so expert at concealing gems they found during their labors, and at passing them on to illicit diamond buyers—known throughout the trade as IDBs—that only about half the diamonds from the Kimberley mines ever reached the strongboxes of the mine owners. The authorities of the Protectorate of Griqualand West—the administrative district in which Kimberley was located—had established a special court to try cases of gem theft and had organized a police force to track down the thieves and IDBs, but their efforts were largely ineffective.

IDBs seldom took a stolen gem directly from a digger. Instead, they would sometimes bury money (or a powerful drug called dagga, which many workers valued even more) near the mines; the diggers, in turn, would bury the stones they had taken. The parties would then conclude a deal by letting each other know where the respective caches could be found. The two nearby Boer republics—the Orange Free State and the Transvaal—paid little note to diamond theft. The IDBs who managed to smuggle stolen stones out of Griqualand West, by hiding them in shotgun shells, canes or rifle barrels, by sewing them into clothing or by concealing them in hollow heels of shoes, had nothing more to fear from the authorities.

Once in control of South African mining, Rhodes set out to stop diamond smuggling at its source. He instituted a system whereby tribesmen recruited for work in his mines were confined in sealed compounds for the duration of their contracts—from three to six months. Merchants in Kimberley protested the loss of trade, but De Beers officials piously answered

Under a supervisor's watchful eye, sorters using sieves classify rough diamonds according to size, shape and clarity at the De Beers office around the turn of the century.

After a day in the Kimberley mines a worker is subjected to a body search that includes even the spaces between his toes. Such scrutiny — and severe punishment for those found smuggling diamonds — slowed but did not stop the lucrative traffic in illicit gems.

that they were saving their laborers from the evils of poisonous liquor. On returning to their compounds in the evening, diggers were expertly searched by guards who ran fingers through their hair, examined all body cavities and ordered them to raise their arms, spread their fingers and jump up and down to shake loose any diamonds they might be concealing.

During the last week of a worker's service he was confined to a hut, with no clothing and with his hands encased in heavy leather mittens resembling boxing gloves. If the man did not make a daily trip to the toilet, wrote South African author Stuart Cloete, "he was given a cathartic. The toilets were so arranged that water flowed constantly through them across sieves of various sizes, and thousands of diamonds that the natives had swallowed were thus retrieved. In spite of these precautions, the natives still managed to steal some stones. They would slash open their legs and conceal the diamonds in the open wounds. The company doctors, by probing any wounds or swellings, recovered many fine stones, for only the finest were worth such self-inflicted anguish." These harsh measures succeeded to the extent that Rhodes was able to abandon a realistic but embarrassing system he had been using to reduce his losses — using undercover agents to buy his own diamonds back from his own diggers.

Rhodes's fortune began to mushroom. He had already sunk vertical shafts on the flanks of the De Beers pipe, tunneling into the blue ground from below the surface as Barnato had done at Kimberley. Now, amalgamation led to even wider application of the more efficient mining technique. The new De Beers Consolidated reduced the cost of producing diamonds to 10 shillings a carat and because of the reduced competition was able to increase the selling price to 30 shillings — up from a previous high of 20.

Rhodes's reluctant ally, Barnato, also grew richer, earning royalties of between £300,000 and £400,000 a year. With his new wealth he hurried off to Johannesburg, in the Transvaal, to get in on the fabulous new gold discoveries made at a spot known as the Witwatersrand, or white-water ridge — called the Rand for short. There he invested in mining claims and real estate in a frantic attempt to gain the sort of mastery he had been denied at Kimberley. Over many years, the strain of managing his affairs in the gold fields drove Barnato to episodes of mental instability. While en route from Africa to England aboard the steamship *Scot* in June of 1897, he killed himself at the age of 44 by jumping into the sea.

Unlike Barnato, Rhodes showed little interest in the Rand at first and had to be goaded by his associates into buying gold claims. Gold simply did not have the same appeal for him as diamonds. He never gave his gold holdings top priority or tried to achieve dominance in the Rand, although he eventually came to be one of the biggest mine owners and, ironically, made a great deal more money from gold than he ever did from diamonds.

Even before winning the Kimberley Central fight, Rhodes had turned his obsessive energy to the advancement of his underlying mission — bringing Africa into the British Empire. Constantly reminded of his weak heart by a throbbing aneurism in one wrist, he was certain that his remaining time on earth would be brief and worked all the harder to reach his goals. His zeal imbued him with high personal courage. In 1884 he traveled alone to a settlement of armed and angry Boers who disputed Britain's claims to Bechuanaland, a large area on the western borders of the two Boer republics. He was confronted at one point by an enraged farmer who reached for his pistol, shouting, "Blood must flow!"

"Give me my breakfast first," said Rhodes, "and then we can talk about blood." Abashed at having forgotten traditional Boer hospitality, the man took Rhodes to his farm, put him up for a week and eventually asked him to be godfather to one of his grandchildren.

In 1889 Rhodes applied to the politics of empire the same kind of cunning he had used to win control of the diamond mines; he contrived a new instrument of imperialism, the British South Africa Company, and won government approval of a charter that gave it broad authority not only to mine diamonds and gold, but to colonize and govern new lands. With his untold wealth and the powers of what came to be known simply as the Chartered Company, Rhodes was the predominant figure in the Cape Colony. When the Cape's government fell in 1890, he became Prime Minister. He now possessed the economic, political and physical base from which the British South Africa Company could launch its quest for territory.

Lured irresistibly by the northern territories of Matabeleland and Mashonaland, he embarked on a series of dubious plots designed to bring them under the control of the Chartered Company. Great areas of this region were dominated by a king named Lobengula, a huge man also known by his admiring people as Drinker of Blood, Calf of the Black Cow, Man-eater and Lion. The King was not only powerful but rich; he owned half a million cattle and two biscuit tins filled with smuggled diamonds brought to him by subjects he had allowed to toil in the mines at Kimberley.

Even before setting up the Chartered Company, Rhodes had managed to wheedle from Lobengula a treaty giving Rhodes the mineral rights to the King's territory. Now the company recruited hundreds of white settlers to pour into Lobengula's domain by promising them large plots of free land, in complete disregard of the limits of the mining treaty. The King, angered but restrained, ordered his warriors not to touch the white invaders. But a band of settlers killed several of Lobengula's subjects, and Rhodes used the incident as a pretext for starting a war in which the company's mercenaries mowed down Lobengula's men by the hundreds with machine guns.

A massive steam-powered winding engine exemplifies the modernization of mining at Kimberley just before 1900. Its steel ropes could lift 9,600 pounds of blue ground 1,000 feet up the mine's main shaft in 30 seconds. The engine was imported from London, the coal to fuel it from Wales.

Lobengula fled northward toward the Zambezi River with his three sons and a few followers, and he soon died—some said from smallpox, others claimed by his own hand. His biscuit tins of diamonds, believed to be worth about five million pounds, vanished with him and were sought for decades afterward by fortune hunters.

The acquisition of Lobengula's territory brought Rhodes to the zenith of his career. He was regarded worldwide—even by the Germans and the Portuguese, who had their own colonial aspirations in Africa—as the supreme empire builder. The British Post Office certified his eminence by ordering mail for the new colony to be addressed to "Rhodesia." Rhodes was exultant: "Has anyone else," he cried, "had a country called after their name?" But his hubris, fueled by his victory over Lobengula, was about to bring him down.

Rhodes had always admired the Boers for their dedication to the soil and their self-sufficiency. He particularly admired their dour patriarch, Ste-

phanus Johannes Paulus Kruger, President of the Transvaal Republic, who was affectionately known as Oom Paul. But none of this kept Rhodes from wanting to lead the independent Boer republics into the British Empire — particularly after he became a big shareholder in the Rand gold mines.

Rhodes was firmly blocked in his repeated attempts to expand his mineral rights in the Transvaal into a federation of governments under the Union Jack. "He goes too fast for me," said the obdurate Kruger. "He never sleeps and does not smoke and has robbed me of the north." Feeling increasingly pressed for time, Rhodes in 1894 decided to achieve his ends with force — by engineering a gold miners' coup d'état in Johannesburg, with the help of an invading army led from Bechuanaland by his friend Leander Jameson.

When the hour for the uprising finally came, in December of 1895, everything went wildly wrong. President Kruger of the Transvaal Republic was alerted — one of Jameson's troopers who was supposed to cut the telegraph line to Johannesburg got drunk and snipped a strand of barbed-wire fencing instead — and Kruger's armed farmers ambushed the 500 attackers, killing 16 of them and capturing nearly all the rest. The Johannesburg miners' revolution was quickly snuffed out, and what came to be known as the Jameson Raid became the scandal of Europe. Several of the participants were convicted by a Boer court and sentenced to death — but Kruger substituted enormous fines, which Rhodes promptly paid. Suddenly a mortal embarrassment to the Empire he had so fervently espoused, Rhodes was forced to resign as Prime Minister of the Cape Colony and exerted little political influence in either South Africa or Britain thereafter.

Rhodes's faith in the Empire never wavered, however, and the last of his many wills established a trust fund to support Rhodes Scholarships for students from British colonies, the United States and Germany. He made them available regardless of race or religion and hoped the scholars would form "an attachment to the country from which they have sprung." Yet even in this philanthropy Rhodes managed to display the curious workings of his contradictory mind: Late in life, talking once about the list of desirable traits required of candidates for his scholarships, Rhodes disparaged academic attainments as promoting "smugness," labeled athletic accomplishments "brutality" and said such qualities as love of truth, devotion to duty, sympathy for the weak, kindliness and unselfishness led to "unctuous rectitude." Only one requirement — leadership — escaped his redefinition.

Rhodes would not have earned one of his scholarships — he lacked too many of the qualities he disparaged. But leadership he had in supreme measure, and he used this trait to lay the foundations for a global diamond monopoly that has endured for most of a century and has made tiny chunks of crystallized carbon seem to all the world to be innately precious things.

Rhodes died in 1902 — with Jameson holding his hand — at Muizenberg, a fishing village near Cape Town where he had recently bought a seaside cottage. "So little done," he murmured at the end, "so much to do." He was not talking about the diamond business: "The only trouble with regard to the industry," he had told his shareholders in 1896, "is that it is becoming a matter of course and uninteresting. It goes like clockwork." But it soon ceased to go like clockwork, and Rhodes's successors at De Beers were left to cope with a phenomenon that has beset them ever since — new floods and yet more new floods of diamonds that threatened to wash away the very foundations of their monopoly. Ω

GARNERING A BILLION-DOLLAR HARVEST

The growl of enormous earthmovers and the whine of power tools signal the transformation of diamond mining from its original helter-skelter of individual prospecting into a four-billion-dollar heavy industry. The annual output of more than 40 million carats — mined in 21 countries, 12 of which are in southern Africa — is harvested from three primary sources: vertical pipes of volcanic ore, alluvial river bottoms and, more recently, remote stretches of ocean beach. Each kind of deposit presents its own problems of engineering and excavation.

An open pit like the one at left marks the top of a mother lode of diamond-studded kimberlite, or blue ground. As digging proceeds, the earth around the pit is cut away in broad terraces called benches, reducing the threat of landslides that plagued the earliest open-pit mines. Terracing also provides a spiral highway for moving men and machinery to the mine floor and for hauling out ore.

Even with terracing, open-pit mining is practical only to certain depths. Beyond about a thousand feet, sophisticated underground mining techniques are required. Shafts as much as a mile deep are driven parallel to the kimberlite pipe, and from them horizontal tunnels are dug to reach the ore.

Retrieval of diamonds is less of a problem in riverbeds whose streams are dry or have been diverted. Here mobile equipment is employed to wash away centuries of silt and probe the craggy bottoms for diamond-bearing gravel.

The ultimate challenge in excavation occurs along a narrow strip of African shoreline near the point where the Orange River pours into the South Atlantic. The first diamond found there, in 1908, was simply picked up off the beach, but most of the deposits are buried under 30 to 60 feet of sand.

To remove the sand and the diamondiferous gravel beneath it requires one of history's largest concentrations of earthmoving machines — 300 giant scrapers, bulldozers, backtrenchers, trucks and even a huge mobile vacuum cleaner. For every pound of diamonds recovered, 150 million pounds of waste must be removed. But the high quality of the gems, all survivors of the long river journey from the inland kimberlite pipes, makes the effort worthwhile.

A dump truck hauls ore to the top of the carefully terraced 45-acre pit of the Finsch mine, South Africa's largest producer of gem diamonds. The 20-ton load of kimberlite will yield an average of 14 carats.

At the Premier mine near Pretoria, formerly an open pit, miners operate air-powered drills in a chalk-marked tunnel 1,400 feet belowground. When undercut from below, the kimberlite breaks up and is hauled by train and conveyor belt to a pulverizing machine before being lifted by elevator up the mine's main shaft.

Taking advantage of Venezuela's dry season, a miner wielding a powerful hose washes away layers of overburden in a dry riverbed to get at the alluvial gem deposits below.

In the diamond-rich Luana region of Angola, a mobile crane hoists a load of promising gravel dug from a deep natural cavity in the bottom of a river whose course has been diverted.

The Atlantic Ocean presents a menacing backdrop to a mining operation on a beach near the mouth of the Orange River in Namibia. Bulldozers and hydraulic excavators strip the sand from the beach (*right*), and the diamondiferous rock beneath is hauled to nearby crushing plants. But no power tool yet devised is as thorough as a hand-wielded brush (*above*) for sweeping the remaining nooks and crannies clean of their last precious grains.

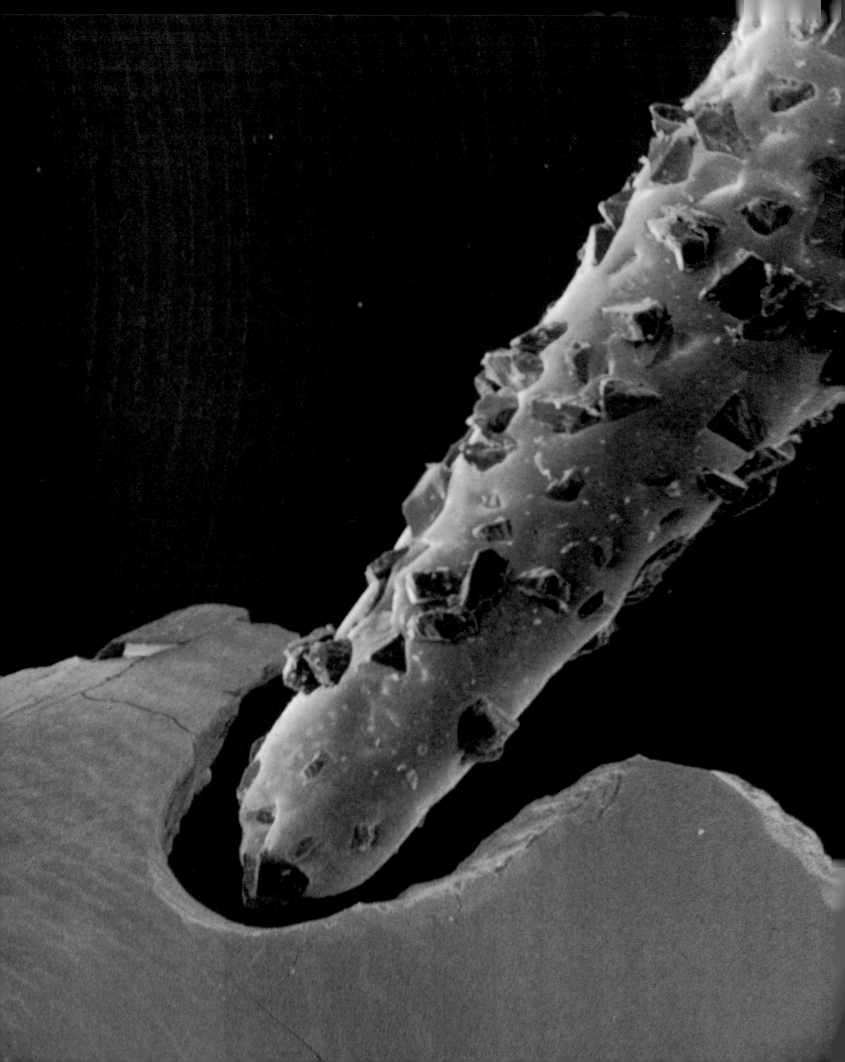

Chapter 5

CONTROLLING A NEW FLOOD OF GEMS

In December of 1902 — nine months after Cecil Rhodes's death, and seven months after the Boer War had at last brought the Boer republics under British sovereignty — a onetime bricklayer named Thomas Cullinan discovered diamonds on a rise of ground near Pretoria, the administrative capital of the Transvaal. Cullinan's little hill proved to be the cap of a new diamond pipe. Within a few years, the Premier mine, as it came to be called, was yielding more gems than were all of the mines controlled by De Beers.

But it was because of a single stone that the Premier caught the imagination of the world. One evening in 1905, Frederick Wells, surface manager of the mine, saw something gleaming in a wall of kimberlite. He opened up his pocketknife and dug out the biggest diamond ever seen. The stone, named the Cullinan, was four inches long, two and a half inches high and two inches across. It was almost as big as a man's fist, and weighed 3,106 carats, or more than a pound. Wells got a bonus of £2,000 for his find, and the Transvaal government bought the enormous stone for £150,000 and presented it as a token of loyalty to King Edward VII.

Had Rhodes still been at the helm of De Beers, he might well have averted the competitive threat from this fabulous new strike by buying the Premier as he had wrested Kimberley Central from his archrival Barney Barnato. But Francis Oats, who had succeeded Rhodes in the De Beers chairmanship, decided that Cullinan had salted his hill with diamonds from elsewhere, and sat back to await the inevitable embarrassment of those who had invested in the mine. Oats was soon to regret his decision. The Premier not only yielded more and more diamonds, but its directors sold them on their own, refusing to cooperate with the London-based Diamond Syndicate set up by De Beers to control the world diamond trade.

Nor was the advent of the Premier mine the only change overtaking the diamond trade of the early 1900s. For Amsterdam, which had monopolized European diamond cutting and polishing for the past three centuries, was relinquishing its grip on the industry. The discovery of gems in South Africa had prompted the revival of another traditional diamond center in Antwerp, Belgium, and had lured Jewish craftsmen, who had long dominated the trade of shaping and selling precious stones, from Russia, Poland and many other Eastern European countries. There were more than 40 cutting and polishing factories in Antwerp by 1900 and two separate trading exchanges by 1904 — all the beneficiaries of steady streams of high quality African diamonds.

Then, in 1907, a Wall Street panic wrecked the American market for

Liberally studded with tiny diamonds, a dentist's drill (magnified 35 times in the photomicrograph at left) cuts cleanly into a human tooth. Drilling is one of the modern applications in which diamonds perform better than any other known substance.

gems, which had accounted for 70 per cent of all diamond purchases. Its sales shriveling, De Beers was forced to cut production and to endure some defections by embittered members of the Syndicate, who went back to selling their diamonds on their own.

Worse was yet to come for Rhodes's successors. Diamonds, it developed, lay littered like spilled peanuts on the deserts of German Southwest Africa's Skeleton Coast — so called because of the bleached ribs of gale-wrecked ships that dotted the shore. A quarter-carat stone discovered by a young African in 1908 was just the first of many thousands to be found lying in the sand near the town of Lüderitz, in what is now Namibia.

Once more De Beers ignored the threat to world gem prices. The company's directors decided that alluvial deposits such as those found in the desert were by nature minor and inconsequential. No one yet understood the process by which diamonds had been delivered to this forbidding resting place — that the Orange River had carried stones from inland pipes to the South Atlantic for millions of years, that a strong current had borne them north along the sea bottom for hundreds of miles and that changes in coastal contours had incorporated these ancient diamond-strewn marine terraces into inland deserts. But German investors soon discovered that they had only to set long lines of African workers crawling over the sand on hands and knees to reap an enormous harvest of gems.

Moreover, because of the long geological sorting process the stones had endured, an astonishing 95 per cent of them were of gem quality. As they were eroded from their inland pipes, carried down the Orange River to the sea and pushed up or down the Atlantic coast by relentless currents, most of the inferior diamonds — those weakened by impurities, fractures or cleavage planes — were ground to dust. Only the finest stones survived to grace the shores of German Southwest Africa, which by 1912 was producing nearly 20 per cent of the continent's diamonds. These gems were sold through a Berlin-based company called the Deutsche Diamanten Gesellschaft. The German company undercut the Syndicate's prices and not only provided dealers in Antwerp with a steady supply of first-rate stones but threatened London's long-standing position as the world center of trading in rough diamonds. In 1914, De Beers finally acted to reassert its authority by agreeing to make the Germans partners in an international cartel designed to control production — and hence prices — once more.

World War I erupted before the plan could be put into effect. Diamond sales withered as the conflict ran remorselessly on, and the trade faced the prospect of yet more anarchy when peace returned. Lingering hostility made German membership in the cartel unthinkable, at least for a time. Furthermore, it had become obvious that diamonds would continue to be discovered in unexpected amounts and places, thus disrupting the lives and fortunes of all concerned. Maintaining the prosperity of the trade despite such exigencies was obviously going to require extraordinary leadership. As it happened, a man with the required ability, the handsome and debonair Ernest Oppenheimer, was already on the scene. Under his guidance the diamond industry would be centralized to a degree that Cecil Rhodes would have envied, and the cartel would maintain its commanding position even as new discoveries were made in distant lands, and even as diamonds were put to industrial and technological uses that were undreamed of until the second half of the 20th Century.

German-born Ernest Oppenheimer, a shy, bookish man with little formal education, enlisted American financial backing to win control of the world diamond cartel. Oppenheimer arrived at the Kimberley mine at the age of 22 with scarcely £50 in his pocket.

Oppenheimer was a study in contrasts. A polite, studious and charming man with a chameleon-like ability to adapt to new situations, he was a German who became a British peer, a Jew who became an Anglican, a self-effacing soul who engaged forcefully in South African politics and, withal, a man of cold nerve and large ambitions.

The son of a Hessian cigar merchant, Oppenheimer in 1896, at the age of 16, followed a family custom — two older brothers having preceded him — when he left Germany for London to work for another German emigrant, a member of the Diamond Syndicate named Anton Dunkelsbuhler. Oppenheimer was fascinated with the stones he handled as a lowly sorter, tried to understand their peculiar characteristics and scrimped to buy an occasional "fancy," or colored, diamond for himself. He also recorded in a series of sixpenny notebooks a great deal of precious information about the trade, gleaned from the company's South African mail.

Oppenheimer's superiors were impressed by his diligence, and in 1902 they sent him to Africa to run the firm's agency in Kimberley. His office adjoined those of several other Syndicate firms, all of which pooled their resources in sorting the diamonds for the De Beers mines and dispatching them to London. As he worked, Oppenheimer was able to meet many of the great men of the diamond trade on their visits to Kimberley, and to gain rare insight into their tactics. And he impressed many of them, particularly after one odd encounter he had with Solly Joel, nephew of the late Barney Barnato and heir to the Barnato empire. Joel one day proudly displayed a huge stone at a meeting of the Syndicate people in Kimberley and asked their opinion of its worth. Everyone at the table scrutinized the stone and named one large sum after another. Finally it came around to Oppenheimer. He kept silent for a long moment, until Joel goaded him to speak up.

"Nothing," said Oppenheimer. "It's not a diamond. It's glass." The surprised Joel asked Oppenheimer coldly if he would wager £50 on the assessment. Oppenheimer hesitated—that was a great deal of money to him—then agreed. A noted gem evaluator later proved him right. Joel's prized stone was a piece of bottle glass that had been ground into the semblance of a diamond crystal by years of washing about in river gravel. Joel paid up, and word of the young man's nerve and judgment spread.

Over the years Oppenheimer prospered, married and was even elected mayor of Kimberley. But his accomplishments were obliterated when anti-German feeling in the early days of World War I drove him and his family into exile in London. War hysteria soon cooled somewhat, however, and Oppenheimer returned to South Africa, where he boldly invested in undeveloped gold fields east of Johannesburg. It appeared that Oppenheimer had abandoned diamonds in favor of gold. In fact, his purpose was to seize control of a diamond industry that was becoming increasingly fragmented.

In the 1880s, Cecil Rhodes had built his diamond monopoly with money borrowed from the Rothschilds' British banking firm. Now, in 1917, Oppenheimer also turned to a mighty financial institution. Having persuaded the noted American mining engineer and future president, Herbert Hoover, to act as an intermediary, he won the backing of Wall Street's powerful J. P. Morgan & Co. For a time, Oppenheimer concentrated his new resources on gold mining, then in 1919 he began to buy up the diamond-rich coastal claims that German investors had started to develop a decade before near the town of Lüderitz. He soon succeeded in amalgamating all the producers in the area into a single concern called the Consolidated Diamond Mines of South-West Africa; before long he was also buying into mines in Portuguese West Africa (now Angola) and the Belgian Congo (now Zaire). By 1923, his widespread holdings had gained him a place in the De Beers-dominated Syndicate.

Then, starting in 1925, the diamond market was jolted by the discovery in quick succession of several new South African diamond fields. Mobs of fortune seekers caused such chaos that the government decided to hold organized rushes, similar to the famous land rush in which Americans had raced for Oklahoma farmsteads in 1889, in order to parcel out claims with a minimum of violence and confusion. At about the same time, prospectors uncovered rich diamond deposits in the sands along the South Atlantic coast near the mouth of the Orange River, in an area called Namaqualand. A horde of gem hunters, many of them representing major mining companies, dashed to the scene, and the world market was flooded with large, handsome stones. Total world production rose to almost eight million carats in 1927, up from 4.7 million just two years before, and more than half of the gems were snapped up by buyers who did not deal with the Syndicate. Prices remained relatively stable, thanks to the great post-World War I economic boom in the United States. But diamond magnate David Harris, a cousin of the pioneering Barney Barnato, reacted with horror to a lavish

The Fabulous Cullinan Find

Squinting into the late-afternoon African sun in January of 1905, Frederick Wells could scarcely believe his eyes. Embedded in the steep earthen wall of the two-year-old Premier mine near Pretoria was the largest diamond that he, or anyone else, had ever seen. Wells, who was the mine's manager of surface operations, scrambled down into the 30-foot pit and used his penknife to dislodge the stone. It filled his hand.

Wells had discovered the Cullinan diamond, named for Sir Thomas Cullinan, the Premier mine's chairman. In its rough form the stone measured 4½ by 2½ by 2¼ inches and weighed 1.4 pounds—an incredible 3,106 carats.

From the moment it was found, the Cullinan was treated as a gem beyond compare. The Premier's owners sold the stone for £150,000 to the government of the Transvaal, which in turn presented it as a token of colonial allegiance to King Edward VII of Great Britain on his 66th birthday, in 1907.

As a precaution against theft, a box purportedly containing the stone was shipped to London amid elaborate security measures, while in fact the Cullinan was quietly sent parcel post bearing a three-shilling stamp.

After a royal consultation, King Edward designated the renowned Asscher brothers' firm of Amsterdam to cut the stone. Once more a ruse was undertaken: The Royal Navy transported an empty box across the North Sea, while Abraham Asscher traveled home with the Cullinan in his pocket.

Awed by the possibility of ruining the great stone, Joseph Asscher studied it for months before attempting to cleave it. Then, on February 10, 1908, he placed a steel blade in a newly made incision and rapped it firmly with his mallet. The blade broke. Only on his fourth attempt did the diamond split—perfectly in two.

Asscher subsequently fashioned the Cullinan into nine large and 96 smaller stones—as well as fragments totaling 9.5 carats. All nine of the majors remain in the possession of the British Crown.

William McHardy, general manager of the Premier mine, holds the Cullinan diamond — the largest ever found — shortly after it was plucked from the mine in South Africa in 1905.

Mallet poised, Joseph Asscher prepares to cleave the Cullinan diamond in 1908. It is said that, after splitting the stone, Asscher swooned into the arms of an attending physician.

Mounted in a British royal scepter (*above, actual size*), the pear-shaped 530.2-carat Cullinan I, or Star of Africa, is the largest of the jewels made from the original Cullinan and is the world's largest cut diamond. Displayed life-sized at left are replicas of all nine of the large diamonds the Cullinan produced.

display of Namaqualand stones: "This will ruin us and the whole diamond trade," he exclaimed. "We are finished."

Ernest Oppenheimer took a quite different view. He already had invested heavily in the new South African fields, and now he simply summoned the prime discoverer of the Namaqualand deposits and bought out his extensive holdings for one million pounds.

Oppenheimer's stature in the industry was growing, as was his certainty that the diamond market must be more tightly managed. He believed that a central organization not only should control as much of the world's diamond production as possible but should try to beat others to the discovery and development of new fields. And De Beers, he wrote, "is to my mind the one institution that should take the lead." Indeed, to Oppenheimer and to many others in the trade, the name De Beers had become synonymous with diamonds.

But the managers of De Beers, who also dominated the Syndicate, remained complacent, basking in past glories and either unwilling or unable to contend with the problems that threatened to undermine their entire operation. To Oppenheimer, by now the industry's predominant figure, the course was clear: If De Beers were to take control of the diamond industry, Oppenheimer would have to take control of De Beers. He gained a seat on the company's board of directors and swiftly consolidated his already considerable position until, in December 1929, he was elected chairman.

Oppenheimer began his stewardship of the Syndicate just two months after the Wall Street crash, amid deepening world depression. The demand for diamonds collapsed, not to revive for many years. The crisis subjected all producers to terrible financial strain, but it also allowed Oppenheimer to extend his control of the diamond trade still further.

In 1930, he dissolved the Syndicate and replaced it with an organization more to his liking—an extension of De Beers called the Diamond Corporation; three years later, he united outside mining operations with those of the De Beers group in an organization called the Diamond Producers Association—whose members pledged to deal exclusively with a newly formed De Beers sales arm called the Diamond Trading Company, or DTC. Taken together, the three groups involved in this arrangement were soon known as the Central Selling Organization, or CSO. Meanwhile, Oppenheimer ceased production at most of the mines controlled by De Beers and directed the trading company to buy up the output of other mines at depressed prices. When the market revived and prices began to rise, he recalled later, "we reaped a golden harvest."

In the years after Oppenheimer moved into the chairmanship—and after his death in 1957, when he was succeeded by his son Harry—the harvests continued to be golden, and De Beers became one of the world's wealthiest and most complex business organizations.

The fortunes of the great cartel depend, just as they did in Cecil Rhodes's time, on myriad crystals of carbon plucked laboriously from their hiding places within the earth. Of the modern ways that have been developed to retrieve diamonds faster and more cheaply, few can match—for audaciousness and sheer drama—the De Beers diamond-mining operation along a 50-mile stretch of the sterile and sun-tortured Skeleton Coast of Namibia (once German Southwest Africa, then administered by South Africa). Ger-

THE BLACK AMSTERDAM DIAMOND
Set off by 15 small brilliants, this 33-carat stone exemplifies the rare colored diamonds that are called fancies. Owned by the Dutch firm of D. Drucker & Son, the pear-shaped jewel appears black because carbon impurities absorb almost all the light that reaches it.

THE SMITHSONIAN PINK DIAMOND
The blushing pink glow of this 2.9-carat fancy, caused by structural strain, makes the diamond especially rare. Found in Tanzania, it is now part of the Smithsonian Institution collection in Washington, D.C.

THE TIFFANY YELLOW DIAMOND
This magnificent cushion-shaped 128-carat gem, mined in South Africa in 1878, is considered an exceptionally fine canary diamond — the connoisseur's term for the stone's intense yellow hue. The tint is an optical effect of the diamond's crystalline structure.

THE EUGÉNIE BLUE DIAMOND
Once owned by Empress Eugénie of France and now in the Smithsonian collection, this exceptional 31-carat heart-shaped gem gets its bright blue color from the presence of traces of nitrogen and boron in its carbon crystals.

mans had harvested their bounty of fine diamonds from surface sands farther to the north before World War I, and prospectors found more at the river mouth thereafter. But later exploration proved that even greater troves were to be found in ancient terraced shorelines now buried under 60 feet of sand along the Atlantic coast.

Through its subsidiary, Consolidated Diamond Mines of South-West Africa, De Beers set out to recover the stones from their ancient hiding places. The gargantuan operation begun in the late 1920s continues today. A fleet of great earth-moving machines roars away, day and night, six days a week, to scrape away 60 million tons of sand a year, exposing the underlying bedrock on which the diamonds have come to rest. The sand is piled up in enormous dunelike dikes along a 10-mile front to hold the Atlantic Ocean at bay a quarter of a mile out from the original shoreline — thus exposing acres of gem-rich gravel terraces that had lain underwater.

The ocean pounds constantly against the sand dikes and can break through them during gales, even though they tower 60 feet high and are 60 feet thick at the base. The earthmovers continually restore any breaches, while giant pumps spew back the intruding water. Behind the dikes the exposed sea floor is divided into sections, each separated from its neighbor by a wall extending inland from the dike. In these compounds, bulldozers scoop up endless piles of diamondiferous gravels and conglomerates, and trucks carry the rubble-like mix to the nearest of four automated treatment plants, where processing and recovery operations are carried out.

After the bulldozers and the trucks have moved on, crews of laborers from northern Namibia — most of whom have worked in diamond fields all their lives — take over. They creep along the bedrock, muffled against blowing sand and armed with little brooms, metal spikes, shovels and dustpans with which they search every cranny for gems that have evaded mechanical collection. They do not shirk; each stone found wins a reward, based on size, that can equal about a month's pay. (An earlier reward scale, based on the number rather than size of the stones found, was woefully counterproductive — anyone who found a large stone was likely to break it into several smaller pieces and thus receive a larger bonus.)

Some 500 miles to the east, in the long-established mines around Kimberley — as in most of the South African diamond mines — the gemstones are wrested from volcanic pipes. In the early days, miners worked these diggings by the tried-and-true open-pit system, but mine operators were soon sinking deep shafts into the rock around the pipes and tunneling into the diamondiferous blue ground by drilling and blasting.

Known as chambering, this method of underground mining has been largely supplanted since the 1950s by a faster, safer and less labor-intensive system called block-caving. In a block-caving operation, miners dig a series of tunnels, or drifts, 400 to 600 feet beneath the top of the blue ground of a pipe. They heavily reinforce the tunnels but leave a number of holes — called draw points — at the tunnel tops. Through these draw points, they then cut funnel-shaped vertical passages upward into the blue ground. Following this operation, the miners hollow out a huge cave, about seven feet high, atop the funnel-like passages. Soon, weighted down by pressure from the mass of blue ground overhead, the roof of the cave begins to crumble and fall through the draw points to the tunnels, from which the material is hauled off for processing. The crumbling continues until all of

A sampler of rough diamonds found in southern Africa demonstrates a startling variety of shapes and shades. The colorless, or "white," stones are the

purest and, with exceptions, are the most valued. The rounder the shape, the longer the gem's exposure to the abrasive effects of running water.

Unglamorous but useful, industrial diamonds, called bort, constitute more than 70 per cent of all diamonds mined. They bring as little as 50 cents per carat when sold as powder for use in commercial abrasives, or as much as $200 for chips used in sophisticated technology.

the blue ground has been drawn off; meanwhile, miners have been tunneling far beneath the original level of operations, preparing for yet another round of block-caving.

Some South African pipes are still mined by the open-pit method. One, the Premier, combines open-pit and block-caving techniques: Ores blasted from the sides of the pit tumble down through funnels and into subterranean collection points for transport to processing plants. But possibly the most ingenious diamond-mining techniques of all are those employed half a world away in the far northern reaches of the Soviet Union.

The Soviets are a fairly recent entry in the diamond industry. Alluvial diamonds had been found occasionally in the country's Ural Mountains as far back as the early 1800s, but no source for them was ever identified. In the late 1930s a young geologist named Vladimir Sobolev observed that a frigid stretch of Siberian territory lying between the Lena and Yenisei Rivers was strikingly similar in its geology to the Kimberley area of South Africa. Both were so-called shields — areas of very old rock that had not been deformed by the movements of the earth's crust. And both had outcroppings of various minerals that were unusual in volcanic formations. Struck by a number of such similarities, Sobolev speculated that diamonds might be found near the two rivers.

Searches during the next decade turned up nothing but an occasional diamond along a riverbank. Then, in 1954, geologist Larisa Popugayeva joined an expedition to the cold and barren wastes of central Siberia, where she discovered a kimberlite pipe that was later named *Zarnitza,* or Dawn. The pipe was not particularly rich in diamonds, but it was just the first of some 400 pipes and seams — including the rich *Mir,* or Peace, pipe — that have been found in the icy Siberian wastelands.

In combat with one of the world's harshest climates, Russian miners at Yakutsk use heavy digging and drilling rigs to extract kimberlite from the frozen Siberian plateau. Discoveries since World War II have made the Soviet Union the second-largest producer of diamonds.

The few pipes that have thus far been exploited are being mined by the open-pit method under the most grueling conditions. Winter temperatures in the area average −50° F. and may go as low as −90° F. At such temperatures nothing behaves as expected — rubber shatters, steel snaps, oil thickens to a gel. Workers are paid a 40 per cent premium over the regular wage in Moscow.

The coming of summer offers scant relief to the beleaguered miners. The pipes are located in an area of permafrost, and even in the warmest months the ground thaws to depths of no more than a few feet. Mining in such conditions requires extreme measures to soften the ground before explosive charges can be laid, and the Soviets have used everything from steam to drills heated by the piped-in exhaust of bolted-down jet aircraft engines. And while summer brings relief from the bitter cold, it also brings mosquitoes in such voracious swarms that the miners must wear veils of netting to protect themselves.

No matter where in the world diamonds are found, or how they are mined, similar methods are used to recover them from the kimberlite or other materials in which they occur. At an average open-pit or underground mine, the ores contain diamonds at a ratio of about 1 part diamond to 18 million parts ore: In order to recover a single ounce of diamonds, or about 142 carats, mining companies must treat 18 million ounces, or 500 tons, of ore. And at the De Beers coastal diggings in Namibia, for example, the ratio is a staggering 1 part diamond to 200 million parts ore.

The purpose of treatment is to reduce the ore into smaller and smaller elements, called concentrates, from which diamonds can finally be separated. At a typical pipe mine, the kimberlite rock must first be crushed to a manageable size, but crushing is seldom required at alluvial diggings because the rock has already been broken down by erosion. The ore is washed and screened in a series of operations that separate the diamonds and other heavier minerals from the lighter, worthless materials. As a final step, the diamond-bearing concentrate is subjected to one of several processes that winnow out the precious stones. One common method consists of running the concentrate in a stream of water over a greased surface: A De Beers employee discovered in 1896 that diamonds cannot be made wet and even after being immersed in water will stick to grease, while the other materials become wet and slide off the greased surface. The diamond-bearing grease is scraped off and melted to release the stones.

Another commonly used technique, developed by the Soviets, capitalizes on the fact that diamonds emit a fluorescent glow when exposed to X-rays. At many treatment plants, diamondiferous concentrates are passed through specially designed X-ray chambers equipped with photoelectric sensors that trigger an instantaneous blast of compressed air to blow glowing diamonds into special containers.

Once the diamonds have been recovered from the tons and tons of gravel or kimberlite, they are cleaned and examined by skilled sorters who separate the gem-quality diamonds from the less-valuable industrial varieties, which are flawed, off-color and unsuitable for jewelry. Such stones were once considered to be waste products, and were even a source of embarrassment to some producers; their primary use was on cutting tools for shaping gem-grade diamonds. But they have become indispensable adjuncts of modern technology since the discovery in the 1930s that only diamond grit is hard enough to sharpen superhard tungsten carbide machine tools. These onetime rejects, known as bort, carbonado or ballas, now make up about 80 per cent of the world's total diamond output and are used by the ton in applications as varied as oil drilling, highway maintenance and telecommunications.

In the recovery plants as well as in the mines, gem diamonds are frequently the target of thieves, and heavy security is a part of every mining operation. At De Beers' Namibian diamond fields, for example, a high barbed-wire fence protects the 50 miles of shoreline from intruders, and anyone seeking admittance to the mining areas is carefully screened. For many years, the company ran the adjacent company town of Oranjemund almost like a prison. No luggage could be taken out without minute inspection, no private cars were allowed in and no furniture, household appliances or company cars were ever allowed to leave — for fear, of course, that hidden gems might leave, too. In 1975, a checkpoint was set up to police the miners when they left the mining area to go to the town, and the controls over the workers' private lives were relaxed.

Although a few gems still trickle through to illicit dealers, most of the world's rough-diamond output is traded through De Beers' Diamond Trading Company. Housed in a fortress-like building on London's Charterhouse Street, the DTC still functions as it did in Ernest Oppenheimer's day. Ten times a year the DTC invites as many as 300 of the world's foremost diamond dealers and jewelry manufacturers to attend "sights" at which each is privileged to buy a box of rough stones chosen and graded ahead of time by the impeccably tailored functionaries of the cartel.

The word "sight" is accurate. The buyers, or sightholders, in attendance open their boxes and inspect the contents before accepting them. They find

A workman scrapes petroleum jelly sprinkled with rough diamonds from a vibrating table in a separating process used at the Premier mine. When the crushed material from the mine is washed over the grease table, the wet gravel vibrates off; but the water slides off the surface of the diamonds, and they stick to the jelly.

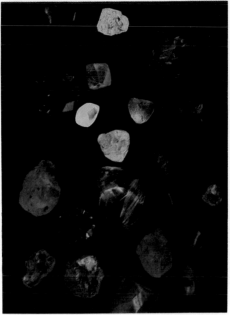

Sorting machines like the one at right make use of the fact that diamonds emit light when exposed to X-rays *(above)*. When crushed minerals pass through a beam, the diamonds' fluorescence registers on a photoelectric cell; the cell triggers puffs of compressed air that eject the diamonds into a waiting container.

that the DTC (which many of them still persist in calling the Syndicate) has given due thought to their particular needs — tailoring the size, shape and quality of the diamonds to the nature of each buyer's market. But De Beers brooks no argument from the buyers about the mix of rough gems (they are graded according to numerous different combinations of clarity, color, crystalline structure and size) or about price, even though the major sightholders may be billed for $20 million and the smallest box will cost at least $150,000.

The buyer can reject the whole box — but as a result may wait in vain for invitations to subsequent sights. In bad times, the dealer is forced to choose between tying up money in diamonds he cannot sell or the awful possibility of being excommunicated if he refuses them.

In most cases, the sightholder buys and hopes for better times, because when diamonds are selling, a De Beers box has immense profit potential. The company raised the price of diamonds 28 times in three decades; a stone that sold for $1,000 in 1949 brought $10,000 in 1980. And De Beers has spent millions to increase the market for diamond jewelry — most memorably with repetitive use of a slogan coined in 1948 by a New York advertising agency: "A diamond is forever."

Today, 80 per cent of the world's rough gem diamonds — including those from a number of countries bitterly hostile toward, not to say at war with, South Africa — go to market through De Beers' Diamond Trading Company. Tons of industrial diamonds are sold through a separate arm of the cartel, as are yet more tons of synthetic industrial stones that it manufactures at plants in Ireland, Sweden and South Africa.

For all their cost, the glassy stones purchased with such formality at a De Beers sight are far from being the glittering jewels the public values so highly. Rough diamonds must be reshaped to increase their beauty and sparkle, and great diamond-cutting and -polishing industries have grown up in a number of cities around the world.

It is a time-tested art; when Amsterdam's master diamond cutter, Joseph Asscher, raised his mallet in 1908 to break apart the fabulous Cullinan diamond *(pages 144-145),* he was repeating a ritual that was at least 500 years old. Indeed, most methods, and even most styles, of diamond cutting had been established by the middle of the 15th Century. Even the brilliant cut, the type most often used to obtain the

A sorter at a Lesotho mine works with diamonds in a locked box that is part of an elaborate system designed to prevent theft. The worker's hands are encased in gloves that are built into the wall of the box.

optimal combination of brilliance and fire from a diamond, made its first rudimentary appearance in the early 1400s in a magnificent jewel called the Three Brethren, fashioned for Charles the Bold of Burgundy. Every advance in cutting and polishing since that time has been merely an improvement made possible by advanced technology and scientific understanding of the laws of optics.

King Edward VII's selection of an Amsterdam cutting house to cleave the Cullinan was the high-water mark of that city's long domination of the diamond-polishing trade. Thereafter, many of the city's best craftsmen moved to the rising diamond center of Antwerp, which in the years after World War I became the premier diamond-cutting city of the world.

A polishing industry also arose in Palestine during World War II, established by a small number of Jewish cutters who had managed to flee the German occupation of Europe. More diamond cutters immigrated to Palestine, and then Israel, after the War, and the industry grew in strength, pioneering a production-line method of polishing in which a single stone goes from one worker to the next, each craftsman specializing in one part of the process. The Israeli industry has carved out a specialized niche for itself in the diamond trade, concentrating on stones classified as melee — diamonds weighing one carat or less in the rough. In dollar value, Israel now trades more polished diamonds than any country in the world.

In recent years one of the most ancient of all national diamond-polishing industries — that of India — has reasserted itself. But far from working on such great stones as the Koh-i-noor or the Tavernier Blue, modern Indian cutters specialize in rough stones so small or of such poor quality that only the country's low labor costs make it profitable to work them. Indeed, India's youthful cutters — many in their early teens — have created a new market for rough that was previously considered suitable only for industrial use. When a sharp-eyed Indian boy or girl can produce a 58-facet round brilliant the size of a pinhead — and earn one or two dollars for the work — the possibilities for finding good material in discolored or flawed crystals increase tremendously.

With varying degrees of success, other countries have tried to establish polishing industries. The Soviets, after a period of producing badly cut gems, now have gained a respected place in the world market for high-quality finished diamonds. New York City, which also received an influx of talented Jewish diamond workers before and after World War II, has its own niche, like Israel and India. Because of its relatively high labor costs, the New York polishing industry has come to specialize in cutting large, high-quality stones.

With the exception of the Soviets, who cut gems mined in their own country, all the major cutting centers rely on the good will of De Beers for their industry's health. Israel's industry is the country's biggest source of foreign currency and employs 10,000 of its citizens, putting an important part of the entire national economy in thrall to De Beers. Staying on the good side of the cartel requires, among other things, that the sightholder refrain from speculating in the gems he has bought at the DTC's quarters on Charterhouse Street. He is expected either to cut them or to sell them directly to other cutters, and not to hoard them or sell the sealed box to another trader for a quick profit.

De Beers is adamant on this point because it knows that the value of diamonds depends largely on their sale to individual consumers as finished jewelry. Any rough gems held by speculators waiting for higher prices will compete directly with the unending flow of new rough from the DTC. The cartel may abruptly cut off a sightholder, no matter how big his past purchases or how old his association with the DTC, if he is caught violating the unwritten but immutable rules.

For the same reasons, the cartel continuously strives to control sources of supply — to discover new alluvial fields and pipes through the efforts of geologists it keeps busy on various continents or, this failing, to make treaties with those who have beaten it to new Golcondas.

Given the frequently volatile politics of sub-Saharan Africa, De Beers must exercise considerable tact, foresight and diplomacy to maintain its paramount position. In 1957, for example, chairman Harry Oppenheimer bought a large Tanganyikan diamond operation from the heirs of an eccentric Canadian geologist who had discovered and exploited the mine, called Mwadui, and who had only recently agreed to deal with the cartel. Seeking to forestall future political problems, Oppenheimer proceeded to turn 50 per cent of the mine over to a government already dominated by blacks. The mine was wholly nationalized when Tanganyika joined with neighboring Zanzibar in 1964 to become the independent nation of Tanzania. But its diamonds, thanks to Oppenheimer's diplomatic gesture, are still sold only through De Beers. The great pipe's riches have begun to run out; miners are finding fewer and fewer gems as they go deeper into the earth. But the cash they earn from the cartel provides the struggling country with one of its few sources of stable income.

Tanzania is not the only developing African nation that depends on De Beers for financial survival. The arid country of Botswana was one

The Ageless Art of Diamond Cutting

Diamond cutting has changed very little in the centuries since Indian lapidaries found that when they ground one diamond against another, both dull surfaces could be made to glisten. The lapidaries had discovered the basic principles of the trade: Because of diamond's hardness, it can be given a surface polish that produces an unequaled luster; because of its power to bend, or refract, light, it can be shaped to radiate great brilliance and "fire."

A modern master cutter may analyze a rough diamond for days or weeks, sometimes making a model of plastic or lead, to find the grain in the carbon crystal and decide how to eliminate or minimize the inclusions that otherwise can reduce the gem's brilliance, and thus its value. After shaping, the gem is polished, a process that increases its flash by creating minute facets, or surfaces, each at optimum angles to those around it.

In the process of cutting and grinding, a stone may lose more than half its size and weight. But with its luminous beauty, a perfectly fashioned smaller jewel can outshine a larger one.

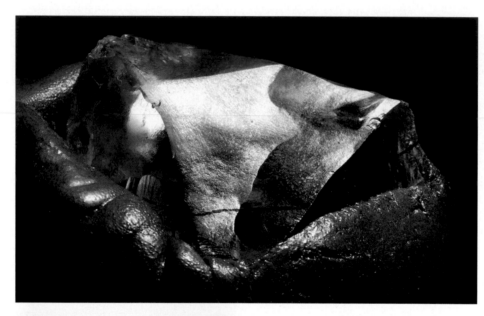

Ready to be cut, a rough diamond is embedded for stability in a dop (from an old Dutch word for "shell") of hardened wax or shellac, and the planes along which it is expected to split are carefully marked in India ink. The stone shown here is the 601-carat Lesotho, one of the largest diamonds ever found.

At the crucial instant of cleaving, a hand-held steel blade inserted in a narrow incision along a diamond's plane line is struck sharply. A misdirected blow from the cutter's rod or mallet can shatter the diamond into rubble.

In a pristine South African factory, white-coated specialists called crossworkers begin the meticulous process of polishing cut stones, which may be as small as 1/10 of a carat.

After sawing, a diamond undergoes a process called bruting, or girdling, in which it is mounted on a lathe and ground by a second diamond. The grinding shapes the gem at its widest point, or girdle; here the result is the round perimeter of the standard brilliant cut.

Sawing, a safer if slower alternative to cleaving, is done with a paper-thin disk made of hardened bronze, coated with diamond dust, that rotates at very high speed. The saw may require several hours to cut through even a one-carat stone.

To create the tiny flat surfaces called facets — usually 58 per stone — that give diamonds their brilliance, the nearly finished gem is held at a precise angle against a spinning, diamond-dusted iron disk — much as a stylus is applied to a phonograph record.

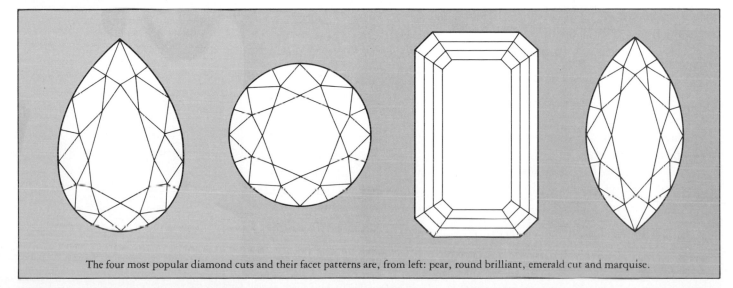

The four most popular diamond cuts and their facet patterns are, from left: pear, round brilliant, emerald cut and marquise.

of the poorest of the Third World countries when it achieved independence in 1966, but its diamond pipes — which the cartel's geologists discovered and developed during 20 years of exploration — are turning it into one of the richest.

Botswana's Orapa pipe, one of three thus far uncovered, is second in size only to Mwadui, and De Beers turns about 70 per cent of the mine's profits over to the government. A fleet of gigantic trucks delivers loads of Orapa's kimberlite to the world's biggest treatment plant by day and night. The mine's riches are reflected by the neat bungalows and wide streets (which are occasionally invaded by lions) and the school, supermarket, hospital, golf course and airstrip that have materialized in the town on the outskirts of the mine.

For all of De Beers' diplomacy and efforts at control, streams of African diamonds still flow into world markets outside the cartel's channels — from countries such as Zaire, the Central African Republic, Ghana and Sierra Leone. These open-market diamonds constitute only a minor part of world production, but their presence dramatizes the difficulties that De Beers continues to face, while their scarcity testifies to the foresight and resolution with which De Beers has operated for so many years.

The company has responded to the recent uncertainties of African politics with a kind of dogged patience, confident that most setbacks will be only temporary. Its holdings in Angolan mines and its control of Angolan production vanished overnight when the Portuguese were driven from the country in 1974 by squabbling guerrilla organizations and Cuban soldiery. Many of the fleeing Portuguese took wine bottles full of diamonds back to Lisbon, where they engaged in complex black-market intrigues. Hordes of illicit diggers descended on the country's alluvial fields, but the new Angolan government took them over in time and resumed doing business with the cartel.

To purchase diamonds from some African nations, however, agents of De Beers must compete with an omnipresent band of Lebanese traders and with buyers from Israel and India. Troops ordered to shoot unauthorized miners sometimes have laid down their rifles to dig for diamonds themselves.

The government of Sierra Leone, for example, shares rights to the country's rich alluvial fields with a British mining concern, but it has not been able to stem invasions by illicit diggers. Some of the world's best gems have turned up in this tropical enclave — including the third biggest ever found, the 968.9-carat Star of Sierra Leone, discovered in 1972 — and scores of traders congregate in the bustling jungle town of Koidu to get their hands on more of them. Other buyers cluster in nearby Monrovia, Liberia.

People also flout the cartel in Europe. Antwerp, host city to the largest group of De Beers sightholders anywhere, is also the location of the world's biggest free market in diamonds. The Belgian government fosters this yeasty state of affairs, remembering that the city became the Continent's preeminent center of gem trading because dealers and polishers flocked there to avoid restrictions in Amsterdam after World War I. Belgium extracts no export or import duties, regards tax evaders and the peculiar bookkeeping methods of its diamond district with magnanimity, and takes a certain bland satisfaction in the arrival of foreigners bent on secret transactions with members of one of Antwerp's four gem exchanges.

A diamond-tipped scalpel makes an ideal instrument for delicate eye surgery. Diamond's unsurpassed ability to take an edge enables it to slice through tissue without tearing it.

Carefully inserted in a metal frame, a diamond wafer becomes a tiny window for the *Pioneer* space probe of Venus. The crystal can tolerate the extremes of heat and cold in outer space.

A key tool in the making of light bulbs, a diamond wiredrawer pulls fiery tungsten from an ingot through a die to produce wire of the minute diameter required.

Unrivaled as a heat conductor, diamond is an integral element in a miniature transmitter's diode (*shown on a fingertip*), used to transmit telephone and television signals.

Many of these dealers are Senegalese, who have established themselves as leading runners of diamonds from emerging African nations, but they rub shoulders on arrival with Arabs, Israelis, Indians and Americans, some of whom fly over from London after attending De Beers sights to shop for bargains.

The Russians operate in Antwerp as well. They bring finished gems produced by their growing polishing industry to be peddled, it is widely assumed, by agents of the KGB. However, despite their official hostility to such capitalistic enterprises as De Beers, the Russians have determined that it is in their interest to cooperate, to a degree, with the cartel. Although Soviet industry is an avid consumer of the country's bort, and its increasing output of polished gems is marketed outside De Beers channels, most of the gem-quality rough stones from Russian mines are sold through the Diamond Trading Company.

Another country that found itself with a rich and growing new diamond industry, Australia, for a time seriously considered becoming independent of De Beers. Diamonds were found in 1978 in the far northwestern part of the continent in an area called, by coincidence, Kimberley. The gigantic Argyle pipe, found in 1979, as well as some large alluvial finds, contains the bulk of an estimated 800 million carats of diamonds, four times South Africa's presumed reserves. The gems are present in enormous quantities and accessible by relatively inexpensive open-pit and alluvial mining; experts believe that Australia could produce up to 25 million carats a year, or 35 per cent of the world's annual diamond production. But gem-quality stones are expected to make up only about 5 to 10 per cent of the Australian yield, compared with the world average of about 25 per cent. Many of the stones found in the country so far are dark brown, about the color of beer-bottle glass. Another 30 to 40 per cent are considered "near gem," the kind of stones from which low-paid Indian polishers can salvage minute cut diamonds. Still, with the tremendous quantities involved, even a small ratio of gems to inferior stones will mean the addition of millions of carats to the world's yearly gem output, the very kind of development that De Beers feels it must control.

The size of the Australian discoveries confronted the cartel with its most serious threat at a time when it was hit hard by a general depression of diamond prices and defections by some diamond-producing countries. After several years of rampant speculation in diamonds by private parties in the late 1970s, prices rose to a wildly inflated level. The inevitable break came in 1980. The price of a bench-mark stone—a one-carat D-flawless (*D* meaning it is as colorless as pure water, "flawless" that it has perfect clarity when looked at under a jeweler's 10-power loupe)—fell from a high of $60,000 that year to just $18,000 two years later. After decades of nudging prices constantly upward, De Beers was unable to prevent this disastrous tumble. And the trading activities of the Russians and the Australians posed still graver threats.

Australian politics entered into the issue. Both the ruling Liberal Party and the opposition Labor Party vied with each other in denouncing De Beers' monopolistic practices and its desire to control an Australian commodity. But Australia had no diamond-marketing expertise, and its high percentage of industrial stones posed special marketing difficulties. In the end, a compromise was reached. De Beers, while getting most of Australia's gem-quality rough for sale through the DTC, made unprecedented concessions. The Australians were permitted to retain 25 per cent of their output to sell on the open market, and to use some of the best rough gems to establish a local polishing industry in the southwestern city of Perth. Thus, for at least a time, De Beers managed to avert the prospect of controlling less than a majority of the world's diamond trade for the first time since Cecil Rhodes established his hegemony nearly a century before.

It may be that all the diamonds that will ever exist on earth have already been formed — scientists think that the last eruption of kimberlite took place 30 million years ago — but they certainly have not been found. The Australian discovery will be repeated in the future; somewhere in the thick green jungles of Brazil, for instance, lurk the pipes that fed a sampling of their diamonds into the rivers of Minas Gerais. Yet even if diamonds were to become significantly more plentiful, so long as De Beers retains its grip on the global market it is unlikely that they will ever be seriously devalued.

It is not simply a matter of their price being upheld by the great cartel that husbands their production and trade; cartels, however colossal, are human creations and therefore transitory, especially when compared with the mystical, infinitely enduring qualities that make the diamond the quintessential gemstone. In a real sense it simply does not matter what value, in what currency, some government or organization tries to impose on the twinkling purity or brooding glow of any precious gem; it will always have an innate value to any human privileged to hold it.

"Suspended between heaven and earth for a brief span of time," wrote the internationally known Brazilian gem merchant Jules Roger Sauer, "man can find in the beauty of a rare diamond or emerald or aquamarine those enduring qualities lacking in himself. The inner fire is not of his making, his role is to glorify the eternal." Ω

Roads and terraces carved into the red earth of northern Australia mark the preparation of an open-pit mine designated AK-1, a future wellspring of diamonds. Australia's estimated reserves of 800 million carats are four times those of South Africa.

A GALLERY OF MASTERWORKS

Throughout history, the color, radiance and durability of gemstones have inspired the finest artistic talents of the world. In every civilization, skilled artisans have incorporated gems into their creations, often achieving transcendent beauty, as the sampling of masterworks presented here and on the following pages attests.

Whether they were designed as personal embellishments, as religious symbols or simply to enhance the appearance of commonplace utilitarian articles, the works of gemstone art reflect the nature of the time and place in which they were created. And because in every society gems were believed — until recently, at least — to possess a range of mystical powers, their use in art often was thought to serve the additional purpose of entreating the gods or protecting the owner from misfortune.

Thus an exquisite piece entombed with a noble Egyptian might be intended both as a guarantee of his safe passage to the next world and as a thing of beauty for him to enjoy after he arrived there. Ancient Persians considered precious stones to be the source of much sin and sorrow, created by evil powers to exploit the covetous side of human nature. But that did not prevent the Persians' lavish use of rubies and sapphires to garnish even such ordinary items as bottles.

Though the names of some of the rich and royal owners of gemstone art have endured, the craftsmen who created the masterpieces were little known in their own time, let alone to posterity. Their obscurity is not surprising when one considers that the completion of a single carving, such as the Chinese jade screens on pages 170-171, could represent the work of a lifetime.

A watch becomes an eternal eye observing the relentless passage of time in this setting of diamonds and a single ruby designed by the 20th Century surrealist Salvador Dali.

A winged scarab, the ancient Egyptian symbol of rebirth, forms the centerpiece of an ornate pendant that was buried with the young Pharaoh Tutankhamen in the 14th Century B.C. The scarab was carved from a translucent quartz called chalcedony.

Aztec artists in Mexico fashioned this two-headed serpent of turquoise mosaic with fangs of shell. Probably worn by a high priest during sacrificial ceremonies, the 17-inch-long ornament was taken by Spanish conquistadors from the treasure halls of Montezuma.

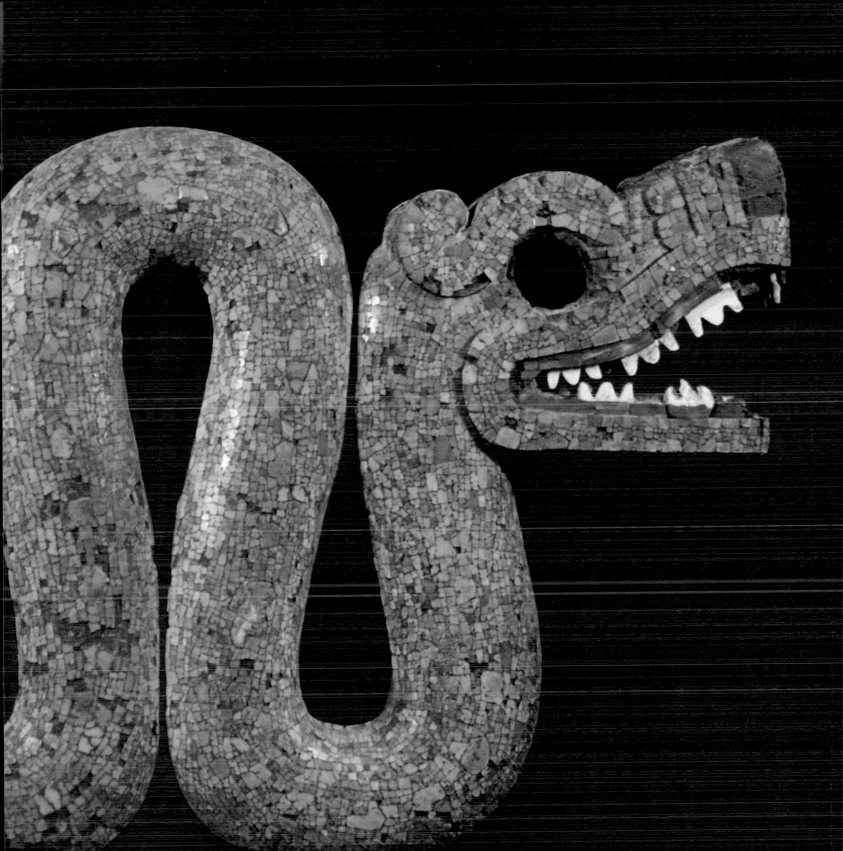

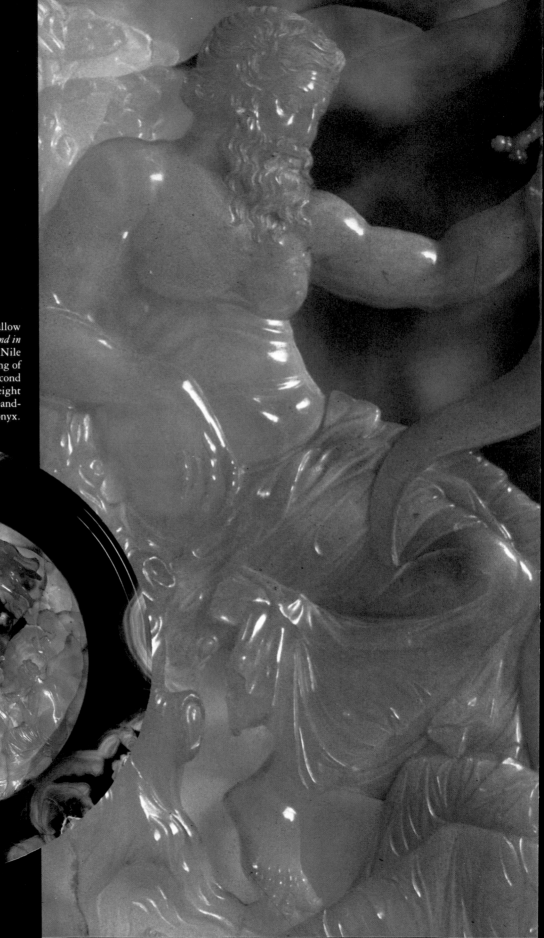

In the exquisitely carved interior of a shallow dish known as the Farnese Cup *(below and in detail at right)*, a bearded god of the Nile proffers the horn of plenty to a gathering of divinities. A Greek artist of the Second Century B.C. cut the cameo, which is only eight inches across, from a multilayered brown-and-white gem mineral called sardonyx.

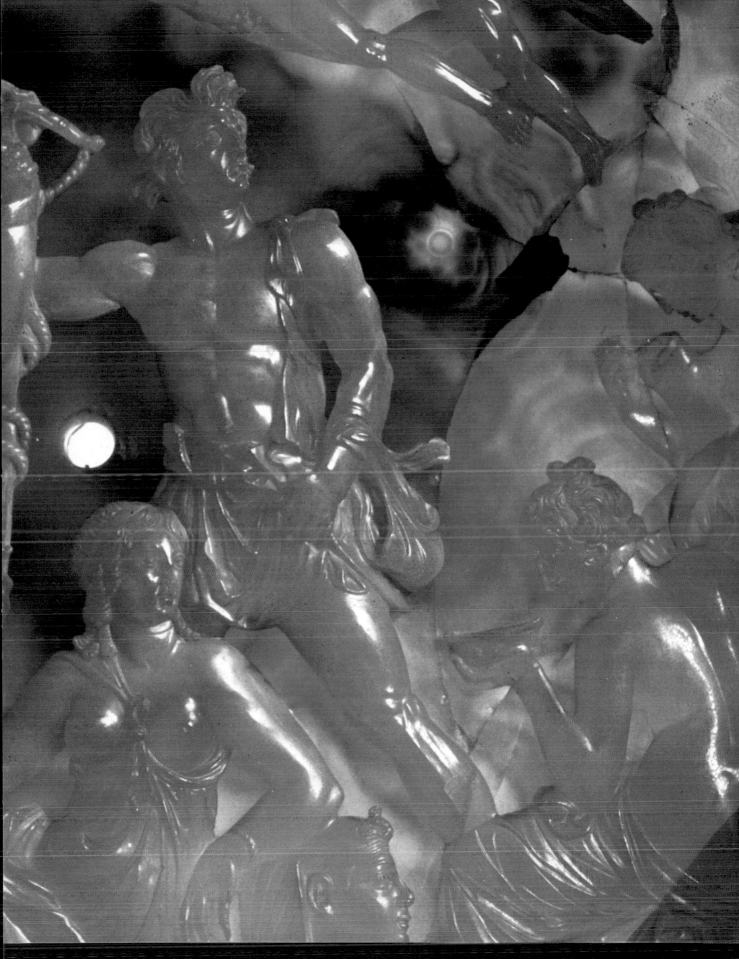

Mogul craftsmen of 18th Century India embellished this jade decanter with rubies and emeralds set in gold. The nomadic heritage of Muslim civilizations is reflected in their lavish decoration of small, utilitarian articles that people could carry with them.

A luminous religious work from Europe's Dark Ages, the cover of the *Lindau Gospels* is a crucifix embossed with clusters of sapphires, amethysts and garnets. The Ninth Century masterpiece symbolized Charlemagne's attempts to revive the glories of Rome in his Frankish Empire.

The loving use of jade by Chinese artisans is exemplified by these translucent screens depicting scenes from the imperial gardens. Less than eight inches high and 15 inches long, the screens were carved from fine Burmese jadeite during the Ch'ing Dynasty.

ACKNOWLEDGMENTS

For their help in the preparation of this book the editors wish to thank: *In Brazil:* Rio de Janeiro — Biblioteca Nacional do Rio de Janeiro. *In France:* Paris — Nelly Bariand; Pierre Bariand, Curator, Museum de Minéralogie, Faculté des Sciences; Dr. John M. Saul. *In the German Democratic Republic:* Dresden — Dr. Joachim Menzhausen, Staatliche Kunstsammlungen, Grunes Gewölbe. *In Great Britain:* London — De Beers Consolidated Mines Ltd. *In South Africa:* De Beers Consolidated Mines Ltd.; Muriel Macey, Kimberley Public Library. *In the United States:* Arizona — (Tucson) Sue Angelon; Peter Kresan; Mr. and Mrs. W. Schupp; California — (San Diego) John Sinkankas, University of California; (Santa Monica) Barbara Dakin, John I. Koivula, Jim Lucey, Gemological Institute of America; Alice S. Keller, *Gems & Gemology;* (Los Angeles) Mr. and Mrs. V. Pelt; District of Columbia — Bob Read, Curator, Department of Botany, Dr. B. Ashley, Dr. Robert Fudali, Chairman, Dr. John S. White Jr., Curator, Department of Mineral Sciences, National Museum of Natural History,

Richard Howland, Special Assistant to the Secretary, Smithsonian Institution; Maryland — (Annapolis) Greg Harlin, Rob Wood, Stansbury, Ronsaville Wood Inc.; (Laytonsville) Joel Arem; (Silver Spring) A. Bonanno, Columbia School of Gemology; Massachusetts — (Boston) S. Sydney DeYoung; (Cambridge) Dr. C. S. Hurlbut, Harvard University; New York — (New York) Joyce McClure, Manager, Belinda Sym-Smith, Group Assistant, Diamond Information Center; Joseph Schlussel, The Diamond Registry; Dr. William Boelke, Morgan Library; Evelyn Owen, N. W. Ayer; Pennsylvania — (Maytown) Lloyd K. Townsend; Virginia — (Alexandria) Maria Estevez; Walter Hilmers; Susan Johnston; Matt McMullen; (Bailey's Crossroads) Mr. and Mrs. L. Walter, Lou-Bon Gems and Rocks; (Burke) Bill Hezlep. *In West Germany:* Idar-Oberstein — Gerhard Becker; Gustav Presser; Konrad Wild, President, Diamant und Edelsteinbörse; West Berlin — Dr. Hans J. Reichardt, Landesarchiv.

Particularly useful sources of information and quota-

tions used in this volume were: *Diamonds: Myth, Magic, and Reality* by Jacques Legrand, Crown, 1980; *Fotoatlas der Mineralien und Gesteine* by Rupert Hochleitner, Gräffe und Unzer, Munich, 1981; *The Gem Kingdom* by Paul Desautels, Grosset & Dunlap, 1971; *Gems Made by Man* by Kurt Nassau, Chilton, 1980; *Gems: Their Sources, Descriptions and Identification* by Robert Webster, Butterworths, 1975; *Gemstones of the World* by Walter Schumann, transl. by Evelyne Stern, Sterling Publishing, 1977; *Handbook of Gem Identification* by Richard T. Liddicoat Jr., Gemological Institute of America, 1981; *An Introduction to the World's Gemstones* by E. H. Rutland, Hamlyn, London, 1974; *Le Monde Merveilleux des Pierres Précieuses à l'État Naturel* by Pierre Bariand, Éditions Minerva, S.A., Geneva, 1979; *Mineralogy* by John Sinkankas, Van Nostrand Reinhold, 1964; *The National Museum of Natural History* by Philip Kopper, Harry N. Abrams, 1982.

The index was prepared by Gisela S. Knight.

BIBLIOGRAPHY

Books

Anderson, B. W., *Gemstones for Everyman.* Van Nostrand Reinhold, 1976.

Arem, Joel E.:
Color Encyclopedia of Gemstones. Van Nostrand Reinhold, 1977.
Gems and Jewelry. Bantam Books, 1975.
Man-Made Crystals. Smithsonian Institution Press, 1973.

Bariand, Pierre:
Le Monde Merveilleux des Minéraux. Geneva: Éditions Minerva, S.A., 1976.
Le Monde Merveilleux des Pierres Précieuses à l'État Naturel. Geneva: Éditions Minerva, S.A., 1979.

Bauer, Max, *Precious Stones,* Vols. 1 and 2. Transl. by L. J. Spencer. Dover Publications, 1968.

Bruton, Eric, *Diamonds.* Chilton Book Company, 1978.

Bury, Shirley, *Jewellery Gallery Summary Catalogue.* London: Victoria and Albert Museum, 1982.

Casson, Lionel:
The Greek Conquerors. Stonehenge Press, 1981.
The Pharaohs. Stonehenge Press, 1981.

Chesterman, Charles W., *The Audubon Society Field Guide to North American Rocks and Minerals.* Alfred A. Knopf, 1978.

Chilvers, Hedley A.:
The Seven Wonders of Southern Africa. Johannesburg: Authority of the Administration of the South African Railways and Harbours, 1929.
The Story of De Beers. London: Cassell, 1940.

Desautels, Paul E.:
The Gem Collection. Smithsonian Institution Press, 1979.
The Gem Kingdom. Grosset & Dunlap, 1971.
Gems in the Smithsonian. Smithsonian Institution Press, 1972.
The Mineral Kingdom. Grosset & Dunlap, 1967.
Rocks and Minerals. Grosset & Dunlap, 1974.

Dickey, Thomas, Vance Muse and Henry Wiencek, *The God-Kings of Mexico.* Stonehenge Press, 1982.

Dietrich, R. V., *Stones: Their Collection, Identification and Uses.* W. H. Freeman, 1980.

Dietrich, Richard V., and Brian J. Skinner, *Rocks and Rock Minerals.* John Wiley & Sons, 1979.

Evans, Joan, *Magical Jewels of the Middle Ages and the Renaissance Particularly In England.* Dover Publications, 1976.

Fisher, P. J., *The Science of Gems.* Scribner's, 1966.

Flint, John, *Cecil Rhodes.* Little, Brown, 1974.

Gascoigne, Bamber, *The Great Moghuls.* Harper & Row, 1971.

Green, Timothy, *The World of Diamonds.* William Morrow, 1981.

Gross, Felix, *Rhodes of Africa.* Frederick A. Praeger, 1957.

Gübelin, Eduard:
The Color Treasury of Gemstones. Thomas Y. Crowell, 1975.
Internal World of Gemstones: Documents for Space and Time. Newnes-Butterworths, 1979.

Hamilton, W. R., A. R. Woolley and A. C. Bishop, *The Larousse Guide to Minerals, Rocks and Fossils.* Larousse, 1981.

Herbert, Ivor, *The Diamond Diggers: South Africa 1866 to the 1970's.* London: Tom Stacey, 1972.

Hochleitner, Rupert, *Fotoatlas der Mineralien und Gesteine.* Munich: Gräfe und Unzer, 1981.

Hocking, Anthony, *Oppenheimer and Son.* McGraw-Hill, 1973.

Hofmann, Fritz, *Rare and Beautiful Minerals.* Exeter Books, 1981.

Hurlbut, Cornelius S., Jr.:
Minerals and Man. Random House, 1970.
The Planet We Live On. Harry N. Abrams, 1976.

Hurlbut, Cornelius S., Jr. and George S. Switzer, *Gemology.* John Wiley & Sons, 1979.

Kirkaldy, J. F., *Minerals and Rocks in Colour.* Poole, England: Blandford Press, 1976.

Kopper, Philip, *The National Museum of Natural History.* Harry N. Abrams, 1982.

Koskoff, David E., *The Diamond World.* Harper & Row, 1981.

Kunz, George Frederick:
The Curious Lore of Precious Stones. Dover Publications, 1941.
Gems and Precious Stones of North America. Dover Publications, 1968.

Lange-Mechlen, Susann, *Diamanten: Edelsteinbrevier.* Stuttgart and Zürich: Belser Verlag, 1982.

Legrand, Jacques, *Diamonds: Myth, Magic, and Reality.* Crown, 1980.

Liddicoat, Richard T., Jr., *Handbook of Gem Identification.* Gemological Institute of America, 1981.

Lockhart, J. G., and C. M. Woodhouse, *Cecil Rhodes: The Colossus of Southern Africa.* Macmillan, 1963.

Ludman, Allan, *Physical Geology.* McGraw-Hill, 1982.

Lye, Keith, *Minerals and Rocks.* Arco, 1980.

Macdonald, Gordon A., *Volcanoes.* Prentice-Hall, 1972.

Mason, Anita, *The World of Rocks and Minerals.* Larousse, 1976.

Mather, Kirtley F., *Beneath Us the Earth.* Random House, 1975.

Meen, V. B., and A. D. Tushingham, *Crown Jewels of Iran.* Toronto: University of Toronto Press, 1968.

Metz, Rudolf, *Antlitz Edler Steine.* Stuttgart: Chr. Belser Verlag, 1978.

Mitchell, Richard Scott, *Mineral Names: What Do They Mean?* Van Nostrand Reinhold, 1979.

Mueller, Conrad G., Mae Rudolph and the Editors of *Life, Light and Vision.* Time Inc., 1966.

McCarthy, James Remington, *Fire in the Earth: The Story of Diamonds.* Harper & Brothers, 1942.

Nassau, Kurt, *Gems Made by Man.* Chilton, 1980.

O'Donoghue, Michael, ed., *The Encyclopedia of Minerals and Gemstones.* G. P. Putnam's Sons, 1976.

Orlando, F. S., *Il Tesoro di San Pietro.* Milan: Rizzoli-Editore, 1958.

Orlov, Yu. L., *The Mineralogy of the Diamond.* John Wiley & Sons, 1977.

Parsons, Charles J., *Practical Gem Knowledge for the Amateur.* Lapidary Journal, 1969.

Patch, Susanne Steinem, *Blue Mystery: The Story of the Hope Diamond.* Smithsonian Institution Press, 1976.

Pearl, Richard M., *Gems, Minerals, Crystals and Ores.* Golden Press, 1977.

Perry, Nance and Ron, *Practical Gemcutting.* Arco, 1980.

Pough, Frederick H., *A Field Guide to Rocks and Minerals.* Houghton Mifflin, 1976.

Prinz, Martin, George Harlow and Joseph Peters, *Guide to Rocks and Minerals.* Simon and Schuster, 1977.

Putnam, William C., *Geology.* Oxford University Press, 1971.

Rhodes, Frank H. T., *Geology.* Golden Press, 1972.

Roberts, Willard Lincoln, George Robert Rapp Jr. and Julius Webster, *Encyclopedia of Minerals.* Van Nostrand Reinhold, 1974.

Rutland, E. H., *An Introduction to the World's Gemstones.* London: Hamlyn, 1974.

Sauer, Jules Roger, *Brazil: Paradise of Gemstones.* Jules Roger Sauer, 1982.

Scalisi, Philip, and David Cook, *Classic Mineral Localities of the World.* Van Nostrand Reinhold, 1983.

Schumach, Murray, *The Diamond People.* W. W. Norton, 1981.

Schumann, Walter, *Gemstones of the World.* Transl. by Evelyne Stern. Sterling, 1977.

Shackley, Myra, *Rocks and Man.* St. Martins Press, 1977.

Shaub, Benjamin M., *Treasures from the Earth: The World of Rocks and Minerals.* Crown, 1975.

Sinkankas, John:
Emerald and Other Beryls. Chilton, 1981.

Gem Cutting: A Lapidary's Manual. Van Nostrand Reinhold, 1962.

Mineralogy. Van Nostrand Reinhold, 1964.

Prospecting for Gemstones and Minerals. Van Nostrand Reinhold, 1970.

Standard Catalog of Gems. Van Nostrand Reinhold, 1968.

Sorrell, Charles A., *Minerals of the World.* Golden Press, 1973.

Tavernier, Jean Baptiste, *Travels in India,* Vol. 1. Transl. by V. Ball. Macmillan, 1889.

Uyeda, Seiya, *The New View of the Earth: Moving Continents and Moving Oceans.* Transl. by Masako Ohnuki. W. H. Freeman, 1978.

Walton, Sir James, *Physical Gemmology.* Pitman, 1982.

Webster, Robert:

Gemmologists' Compendium, 6th ed. Van Nostrand Reinhold, 1979.

Gems: Their Sources, Descriptions and Identification. Butterworths, 1975.

Weinstein, Michael, *The World of Jewel Stones.* Sheridan House, 1958.

Weyman, Darrell, *Tectonic Processes.* London: George Allen & Unwin, 1981.

Williams, Gardner F., *The Diamond Mines of South Africa,* Vols. 1 and 2. B. F. Buck, 1905.

Wolf, A., *A History of Science, Technology, & Philosophy in the 18th Century,* Vol. 1. Harper & Brothers, 1961.

Woolley, Alan, ed., *The Illustrated Encyclopedia of the Mineral Kingdom.* Larousse, 1978.

Zucker, Benjamin, *How to Buy and Sell Gems: Everyone's Guide to Rubies, Sapphires, Emeralds and Diamonds.* Times Books, 1976.

Zwierlein-Diehl, Erika, *Antike Gemmen in Deutschen Sammlungen,* Vol. 2. Munich: Prestel Verlag, 1969.

Periodicals

Abraham, Jack S. D., "Heat Treating Corundum: The Bangkok Operation." *Gems & Gemology,* Summer 1982.

Bernstein, Peter W., "De Beers and the Diamond Debacle." *Fortune,* September 6, 1982.

Birmingham, Nan Tillson, "Rare and Royal Rubies." *Town & Country,* June 1980.

Caputo, Robert, "Sudan: Arab-African Giant." *National Geographic,* March 1982.

Chernush, Akosh, "Dazzling Jewels from Muddy Pits Enrich Sri Lanka." *Smithsonian,* June 1980.

Cobb, Charles E., Jr., "After Rhodesia, a Nation Named Zimbabwe." *National Geographic,* November 1981.

Cole, Amy, "From Rough to Ring." *Lapidary Journal,* January 1983.

Darragh, P. J., A. J. Gaskin and J. V. Sanders, "Opals." *Scientific American,* April 1976.

Dolinger, Jane, "Muzo — Mountain of Green Gold." *Rock & Gem,* November 1972.

Farrell, Eileen, "The Australian Wild Card Is Now De Beers' Ace in the Hole." *The Goldsmith,* April 1982.

Gems & Gemology, Vols. 18 and 19.

Green, Timothy S.:

"Buckets of Diamonds: The Precious Pebbles of Kimberley." London: *The British Empire,* Vol. 3, No. 29.

"Diamond Diggers in Namibia Sift Ocean Sands for Gemstones." *Smithsonian,* May 1981.

Gübelin, E., "The Ruby Mines of Mogok, Burma." *Lapidary Journal,* June 1966.

Hodgson, Bryan, "Namibia: Nearly a Nation?" *National Geographic,* June 1982.

Hoge, Warren, "Colombia's Emeralds Leave Many Rich, Many Dead." *The New York Times,* November 19, 1980.

Jeweler/Gem Business, January-February 1983.

Jordan, Robert Paul, "Sri Lanka: Time of Testing for an Ancient Land." *National Geographic,* January 1979.

Keller, Peter C.:

"The Chanthaburi-Trat Gem Field, Thailand." *Gems & Gemology,* Winter 1982.

"Emeralds of Colombia." *Gems & Gemology,* Summer 1981.

Kovac, Cyril, "Queenland's Sapphires." *Lapidary Journal,* November 1974.

Kurtis, Bill, "A Worldwide Scramble for the Rarest Rubies." *The New York Times,* November 8, 1981.

Murray, Donald G., "Sapphire Town, Australia." *Gems & Minerals,* February 1977.

Nassau, Kurt:

"The Causes of Color." *Scientific American,* October 1980.

"Cubic Zirconia: An Update." *Gems & Gemology,* Spring 1981.

Nordland, Rod, "On the Treacherous Trail of the Rare Ruby Red." *Asia,* October 1982.

"Preparing to Aid the Free State." *South,* January 1982.

Simon, Karl Günter, "Deutschlands Hauptstadt der Karate." *Geo,* May 1983.

Sobolev, N. V.:

"Scientist Forecast Siberian Diamond Finds." *Diamond News and S. A. Jeweller,* Vol. 44, No. 8, 1981.

"Siberian Diamonds — Minerals from the Earth's Mantle." *Indiaqua* 26, 1980/3.

Stevens, Jane Perham, "The Gerhard Becker Miniatures in Maine Tourmaline." *Lapidary Journal,* January 1979.

Switzer, George S., "Questing for Gems." *National Geographic,* December 1971.

Ward, Fred, "The Incredible Crystal Diamonds." *National Geographic,* January 1979.

Willard, Helen M., "The Yogo Sapphire, Montana's Elusive Treasure." *Lapidary Journal,* July 1981.

Wilson, Arthur Norman, "Siberian Treasures: The Most Remarkable Diamond Regions on Earth." *Jeweler's Circular-Keystone,* February 1982.

Zwaan, Peter C., "Sri Lanka: The Gem Island." *Gems & Gemology,* Summer 1982.

Other Publications

Annual Report to 31st December 1982, De Beers Consolidated Mines Limited, Kimberley, South Africa.

International Gemological Symposium Proceedings 1982, Gemological Institute of America. Selected articles:

Baron, Arnold A., "The Yogo Sapphire."

Sauer, Daniel A., "Emeralds From Brazil."

Shire, Maurice, "Emeralds."

Wilson, Arthur Norman, "The Origin of Diamonds."

PICTURE CREDITS

The sources for the illustrations that appear in this book are listed below. Credits for the illustrations from left to right are separated by semicolons; from top to bottom the credits are separated by dashes.

Cover: Harold and Erica Van Pelt © 1981, courtesy Collection of Keith Proctor. 6, 7: Chip Clark, Smithsonian Institution; Joel E. Arem. 8: Dane Penland, courtesy Smithsonian Institution — Harold and Erica Van Pelt © 1982, courtesy Perkins Sams' Collection. 9: Harold and Erica Van Pelt © 1981, courtesy Art Sexauer; Harold and Erica Van Pelt © 1981, courtesy Smithsonian Institution. 10: Breck P. Kent © — Harold and Erica Van Pelt, courtesy J. and E. Greenspan. 11: Harold and Erica Van Pelt, courtesy Bill Larsen (2) — Harold and Erica Van Pelt, courtesy Colin Curtis; Harold and Erica Van Pelt, courtesy Pala International. 12, 13: Nelly Bariand, Paris — Harold and Erica Van Pelt © 1983, courtesy Romney Hayden Satish Patel; Harold and Erica Van Pelt © 1981, courtesy Alex Blythe; Michael Havstad, courtesy Gemological Institute of America. 14: Nelly Bariand, Paris — Lee Boltin ©. 15: Harold and Erica Van Pelt, courtesy Collection of Los Angeles County Museum of Natural History; Harold and Erica Van Pelt © 1981, courtesy Kristalle — Harold and Erica Van Pelt, courtesy J. and E. Greenspan (2). 16: Harold and Erica Van Pelt © 1981, courtesy Collection of Banco De La Republica, Bogota, Colombia; Tino Hammid, courtesy Gemological Institute of America. 17: Harold and Erica Van Pelt © 1981, courtesy Collection of Keith Proctor, upper right, Lee Boltin ©. 18, 19: Harold and Erica Van Pelt, courtesy of J. and E. Greenspan — Harold and Erica Van Pelt, courtesy J. and E. Greenspan; Harold and Erica Van Pelt; Dane Penland, courtesy Smithsonian Institution. 20: Michael Holford, London. 22: Jean-Loup Charmet, courtesy Bibliothèque Nationale, Paris — © VNU Books International, courtesy Bibliothèque Nationale, Paris. 25: Chip Clark, Smithsonian Institution. 26: Fred Ward from Black Star ©. 27: Map by Bill Hezlep. 29: Kay Chernush ©. 30: Roloff Beny, Rome. 31: Konrad Helbig ©/ZEFA, Dusseldorf. 32: Robert W. Read — Francesco Venturi/Ricciarini, Milan; Kay Chernush ©. 35: Dane Penland, courtesy Smithsonian Institution © 1978. 37: © VNU Books International, courtesy Biblioteca Nacional do Rio de Janeiro, Brazil. 38: Chip Clark, Smithsonian Institution. 40-49: John I. Koivula. 50: Courtesy Gemological Institute of America. 52: British Crown Copyright, reproduced with the permission of the Controller of Her Britannic Majesty's Stationery Office. 54: Nelly Bariand, Paris. 58: Art by Rob Wood. 59: Art by Rob Wood (3); Dane Penland, courtesy Smithsonian Institution (2) — Dane Penland, courtesy Smithsonian Institution © 1978. 60: Art by Rob Wood (2); Dane Penland, courtesy Smithsonian Institution — Dane Penland, courtesy Smithsonian Institution © 1980. 61: Art by Rob Wood (3); Joel E. Arem (2) — Dane Penland, courtesy Smithsonian Institution. 63: Maurice van Horn, courtesy Eastman Kodak Company. 65: Chip Clark, Smithsonian Institution (2) — Lee Boltin ©. 66: Dane Penland, courtesy Smithsonian Institution — art by Matt McMullen. 67: Dane Penland, courtesy Smithsonian Institution © 1977 — art by Matt McMullen. 68: Art by Maria T. Estevez (2) — Joel E. Arem; Chatham Created Gems. 69: John I. Koivula. 72-79: Art by Lloyd K. Townsend. 80: Amos Schliack/Focus, Hamburg. 83: Harold and Erica Van Pelt, courtesy Los Angeles County Museum of Natural History. 84: Harold and Erica Van Pelt © 1981, courtesy Pala International. 85: Breck P. Kent ©. 86, 87: Alan Jobbins, London — Dane Penland, courtesy Smithsonian Institution © 1977. 89: Harold and Erica Van Pelt, courtesy Collection of Allan Caplan. 91: John I. Koivula © 1982 — Dane Penland, courtesy Smithsonian Institution. 92: Don Smetzer © 1981 from Click/Chicago — The Photographic Library of Australia, Sydney. 93: David Doubilet. 94: Kjell B. Sandved; Tom Walker. 96: Charles Moore from Black Star. 98: Harold and Erica Van Pelt, courtesy Irénée du Pont Collection, University of Delaware. 100, 101: Romano Cagnoni from Black Star © 1979. 102, 103: Peter C. Keller. 104, 105: Peter C. Keller, inset, Romano Cagnoni from Black Star © 1979. 106, 107: Romano Cagnoni from Black Star © 1983 — courtesy Kawai; Romano Cagnoni from Black Star © 1979. 108: Romano Cagnoni from Black Star © 1983. 109: Giuseppe Bazzanella/De Pietro Press, Rome. 110: *Punch,* London. 112: Map by Bill Hezlep. 113: J. R. Oldfield, from *Cecil Rhodes,* copyright 1974 by John Flint, published simultaneously in Canada by Little, Brown & Company (Canada) Limited. 114, 115: De Beers Consolidated Mines Ltd. 117: Map by Bill Hezlep — art by Greg Harlin. 118: De Beers Consolidated Mines Ltd.; Kimberley Public Library. 119-121: De Beers Consolidated Mines Ltd. 122, 123: Diamond Information Center — art by Susan Johnston; De Beers Consolidated Mines Ltd. (2). 124, 125: Fred Ward from Black Star ©. 126, 127: Kimberley Public Library; The Mansell Collection, London. 128: The Mansell Collection, London. 129: Photo Harlinque-Viollet, Paris. 131: De Beers Consolidated Mines Ltd. 132: Da niele Pellegrini, Milan. 134, 135: De Beers Consolidated Mines Ltd.; Fred Ward from Black Star ©. 136, 137: Guy Philippart deFoy, © VNU Books International, Paris; René Delville, Bruxelles, © VNU Books International, Paris. 138-140: Fred Ward from Black Star ©. 142: De Beers Consolidated Mines Ltd. 143: Pictorial Press Agency, London. 145: De Beers Consolidated Mines Ltd. (2); British Crown Copyright, reproduced with the permission of the Controller of Her Britannic Majesty's Stationery Office (2). 146: Fred Ward from Black Star © — Dane Penland, courtesy Smithsonian Institution © 1978. 147: Fred Ward from Black Star © — Dane Penland, courtesy Smithsonian Institution © 1978. 148-150: Fred Ward from Black Star ©. 151: A.P.N., Paris. 152-154: Fred Ward from Black Star ©. 156: Charles Moore from Black Star — Lee Boltin ©; Fred Ward from Black Star ©. 157: Fred Ward from Black Star © — art by Walter Hilmers. 158, 159: Fred Ward from Black Star ©. 160, 161: Roger Garwood, Daily Telegraph ©, London. 162: Robert Descharnes ©, Paris. 163: Lee Boltin ©. 164, 165: Irmgard Groth, Mexico City, courtesy Museum of Mankind, London. 166, 167: Museo Nazionale, Naples, photographed by Scala, Florence. 168: Michael Holford, London. 169: The Pierpont Morgan Library. 170, 171: Dane Penland, courtesy Heffernan Collection.

INDEX